'Heartbreaking, powerful, clear-sighted. Powered by the clarity and force of a mother's great love for her children, and the author's reflective capacity honed by years of legal practice and research, this memoir faces fundamental questions about life itself. Hannah Robert experienced an immense tragedy and has given others a true and guiding light.'

Zoë Morrison

'Hannah Robert's *Baby Lost* is a stunning rumination on the minutiae of loss and grief, and the epic struggle involved in putting yourself back together after unspeakable tragedy.

Baby Lost is a courageous and beautiful memoir. With devastating honesty, Hannah offers up her grief, presenting her story with a deft, insightful touch, allowing the reader to bear witness to a loss that is far too often unspoken.'

Monica Dux

'A gutsy, vivid and unflinching book about unspeakable loss. Hannah Roberts's book will resonate with anyone who has known the darkness of grief, and the gradually returning light.'

Hilary Harper

baby lost

baby lost

A story of grief and hope

HANNAH ROBERT

MELBOURNE UNIVERSITY PRESS

MELBOURNE UNIVERSITY PRESS
An imprint of Melbourne University Publishing Limited
Level 1, 715 Swanston Street, Carlton, Victoria 3053, Australia
mup-info@unimelb.edu.au
www.mup.com.au

First published 2017
Text © Hannah Robert, 2017
Design and typography © Melbourne University Publishing Limited, 2017

This book is copyright. Apart from any use permitted under the *Copyright Act 1968* and subsequent amendments, no part may be reproduced, stored in a retrieval system or transmitted by any means or process whatsoever without the prior written permission of the publishers.

Lyrics by Katy Steele (Little Birdy) are reproduced with permission, via Graham McLuskie. Extracts from 'When Things Fall Apart' by Pema Chödrön are reproduced with permission, courtesy of the Pema Chödrön Foundation. Zainab's blanket, pictured on the cover, was knitted and crocheted by Joanna Robert.

Every attempt has been made to locate the copyright holders for material quoted in this book. Any person or organisation that may have been overlooked or misattributed may contact the publisher.

Text design and typesetting by Cannon Typesetting
Cover design by Klarissa Pfisterer
Printed in Australia by McPherson's Printing Group

National Library of Australia Cataloguing-in-Publication entry

Robert, Hannah, author.
Baby lost: a story of grief and hope/Hannah Robert.

9780522869439 (paperback)
9780522869446 (ebook)

Robert, Hannah.
Mothers—Australia.
Fetal death—Psychological aspects.
Grief in women.
Hope.

If the content of this book brings up issues for readers, for help or information call:
SANDS (Stillbirth and Neonatal Death Support): www.sands.org.au
Stillbirth Foundation (A charity raising money for research and education on stillbirth and stillbirth prevention): stillbirthfoundation.org.au
An online community of baby lost parents, which includes resources on how to plan a funeral for a baby, how to help a friend through baby loss etc.: www.glowinthewoods.com
Lifeline: 131 114

Contents

Part I: Impact

1 Sunday, 27 December 2009 — 3
2 The second-best blanket — 15
3 Shavasana — 21
4 The torture booties — 30
5 The crazy lady in ward four — 33
6 Frida and me — 42
7 Tabloid tragedy — 51
8 Permission to bend — 60

Part II: Re-entry

9 Zombieland — 67
10 The 'born alive' rule — 73
11 Sun salute with bedpan — 87
12 The posthumous godfather — 91
13 Matryoshka — 100
14 Histopathology — 106
15 Proof — 110
16 Scar tissue — 118
17 Funeral appreciation — 127

Contents

18	I have a dark-haired daughter	133
19	Dr No-Sperm-for-You	137
20	Heartbeat	144
21	Making the judge cry	147
22	Close up with hope	156
23	The charnel ground	162
24	Fat Tuesday	168
25	Undone	175
26	Tsunami	182
27	Earth and sun	187

Part III: Ripples

28	Both my babies	199
29	Zoe's Law	204
30	Holding the torch	218

Acknowledgements	225
Notes	227

*For Zainab and Mia
and all the other babies gone too soon*

Promises

I will greet you with hands smelling of oranges.
I will kiss your mouth in your sleep.
I will let you surprise me
Over and over again.
I will curse that my hands can't bat away all the things that will
　　hurt you.
I will remember—despite the shock—that no matter how many
　　times I have dreamt you
You are your very own dream
From your very own flickering head.

I will breathe you in and mingle you with my familiar cells.
I will breathe you out and let you mingle amongst the hard
　　and soft particles of the air.
I will bring you home,
And I will open the door.

And as much as I delight
In the still unreal thought
of seeing the light bounce
from your face onto mine
I will not hurry you.

(September 2009)

Part I
IMPACT

1
Sunday, 27 December 2009

There is only one place to start with this story—the point where all the ripples start, the moment of impact. Everything circles around that.

I replay this moment often. There we were, buckled in and travelling north on a suburban arterial road at around 5.40 p.m. two days after Christmas. We were not a conventional family for all kinds of reasons—two mums (one Lebanese, Rima; one a 'skip', me), with Rima's teenage daughters from her previous marriage (Jackie and Jasmin), and our long-awaited donor-conceived baby on the way—but it was the most ordinary of family car trips. We were heading home in the station wagon after visiting my cousin to drop off belated Christmas presents. I was driving, with Rima next to me in the front passenger seat; Jasmin in the back seat on the left, reading her book; and Jackie behind me. She had been leaning on the window gazing out, but leaned forward to ask Rima something.

We'd been listening to the cricket, and I said to Rima, 'Hon, can we change this? Listen to some classical music for Haloumi?' Haloumi was our name for the baby that bulged in my eight-months pregnant belly, that had been hiccuping all morning.

But Rima didn't reply, and didn't change the station, because in front of us we could see exactly what this moment was—in the shape of a four-wheel drive, which had hit the car in front of it in the southbound lane and was now swinging sideways onto our side of the road. I'd started an annoyed query, 'What is he doing?', but finished with a yell, 'FUCK OFF!!'

And I braked. I pushed with my arms and my legs, and the tiny hairs on my arms and legs, to try to push that car away from my family and me, and the little one curled in my belly.

The impact smacked two moments—before, and after—together so forcefully that I was left puzzling about what they were doing next to one another. All I know of it was its loudness, and the shudder it left in our bones. We know it happened, we had the evidence before us, in torn metal pieces and CT scans, but it was too quick—too much to fit into one tiny moment, so that everything broke, and the normal boundaries of our lives split apart.

We stopped moving instantly and I could still hear myself yelling and thought, 'Too late for that,' and shut my mouth so hard that my teeth chipped against one another. I made a decision—this was actually happening, and since I couldn't undo it, I'd better deal with it.

I turned the engine off and looked at Rima—lovely, alive Rima, though she was screaming too by now. I could hear the girls screaming behind us, and though I couldn't turn and see them, I knew they would be hurt but okay.

I looked to my right, where the four-wheel drive had come to a stop, as if we were just parked cars in some wrecking yard. A clear liquid was gushing from the other car's mangled engine. I thought, 'If that's petrol, we could be blowing up any moment now.' I had visions of an action-movie scene—a billow of flame, and bodies moving in slow motion. I couldn't move—the car was crushed in around my legs. 'Rima, get out of the car. Tell the girls to get out.'

Later, in the hospital, Rima mused, 'I opened the car door, but then I realised I was too hurt to actually move. Why did I open the car door?'

'Because I told you to get out. Because I thought the car would explode.'

Sunday, 27 December 2009

I felt calm. I drew great draughts of air and tried to send some of that calmness towards Rima, who was still screaming. My thoughts sliced through the slow-moving time around us. If we could just be calm and reasonable, it would all be okay—the ambulances would come, they would unfold this car around me, my baby might have to arrive a little early but would be okay. Thirty-four weeks—this child would already be so strong. 'Viable'. *Isn't that right, Haloumi?*

•

Seven months before, on a Friday night, I had got off the train from Newcastle, and walked up the hill from Central Station in Sydney's gritty heart and into the pub where Rima was having work drinks.

'Hannah!' Nan and Veronica beamed at me, arms open. 'Here she is!' Rima turned and gave me a bigger smile and a tighter squeeze than usual. And then, in my ear, 'You still feeling nauseous?'

'Yep—still queasy.'

'Good—I'll get you a lemonade then!'

We hugged our secret to ourselves; it was still early days. But we were each allowed to tell one person, and Rima's was Chantal. She found us later that evening, gave me a big hug and whispered, 'So! I hear there's a Mazloumi-haloumi on the way! A baby haloumi!'

I bit my lip and a smile split across my face. 'Yeah—just a tiny little haloumi cheese so far, but definitely a little haloumi!'

I made cryptic Facebook posts: 'I love haloumi cheese' or 'haloumi in my belly!' I fretted about the logistics. Two-and-a-half years before, I'd made the leap from commercial litigator to lecturer at Newcastle Law School—I loved my work, but commuting from Sydney was complicated. I'd just received an offer to move to La Trobe Law School in Melbourne, where I'd grown up, and where my family would be close by. We'd decided on a move, but there was nothing simple about uprooting ourselves.

•

Where the impact had strangely calmed me, it had done the opposite to Rima. She was sobbing, 'My children, my children.' I held her hand; '*Habibi*, please, we are going to be okay.'

'Can you feel the baby move?' She looked at me hard, and asked the question again. I didn't want to answer and engage with the universe of doubt that surrounded it.

'I don't know, my love. I've got a few other issues to think about right now.'

I listed these in my head, concisely and calmly: explosion, being cut out of the car, whether my legs or spine were crushed, Jackie, Jasmin. Inside my body felt calm, safe—it was the outside that was in trouble. Don't worry, Haloumi, I'll get us out of here.

•

When we sat in the obstetrician's office six weeks later for our review appointment, I asked him about the heartbeat the paramedic said he had heard in the ambulance. 'Is there anything on my file about that? Could she still have been alive in the ambulance?'

It took a good twenty minutes on the phone for him to get to talk to the person in charge of the medical records department.

'There's nothing on your file about a fetal heartbeat of 155 in the ambulance. We'll probably never know, but I have to say it took me many years of practice as an obstetrician before I could accurately measure a fetal heartbeat with a stethoscope, so there's a good chance they got it wrong. And, from the look of your placenta when we did the caesar, it had completely abrupted, probably very quickly on impact.'

I sat there looking at the dots on his bow tie and wished I could slap my coolly calm self as she sat in that wrecked car and say, 'Your child is dying right now—anything you want to say to her, you need to say it now.'

•

Sunday, 27 December 2009

In that calm space, it didn't take long for people to come to us. A man appeared at my window. 'I'm thirty-four weeks pregnant,' I told him matter-of-factly.

He said, 'Here, hold this to your head,' and put a cloth in my hand, pressing it against the side of my head above my right ear. It didn't hurt there; it was just warm and wet. He was already on the phone. 'Two women, one of them is thirty-four weeks pregnant'—looking at me for confirmation.

I nodded.

'Are you in pain?'

'I'm okay; I just feel squashed. I can move my toes but I can't get my legs out. I need to be cut out of here.'

I looked down—my legs were pulled up protectively around my bulging belly, my toes flexed a bit further back than I had thought possible. Metal and plastic were bent around my legs, but they felt whole and okay, just trapped. My toes were obediently wiggling—painted toenails (for Christmas), new bronze metallic Birkenstocks bent at angles. 'I'll have to get new Birkenstocks,' I thought.

He kept moving around the car, relaying Rima's injuries to the operator, then Jasmin's, then Jackie's. Another guy, younger, came to my door. 'Are you okay?' he started, and then said, 'Oh fuck.' I could feel the panic sweating off him as he looked at me and the car bent around me. I turned away and looked at Rima instead, letting my calm roll towards her.

•

In the trauma ward afterwards, I listened over and over to a particular song by Little Birdy:

> I haven't seen no place like this
> I haven't seen no place like this
> No one will see, no one will see, what I do now, what I do now, oh it's just us moving

I haven't seen a place so ghost-like
a place that's seen some of the best in my eyes
Pages will turn, sirens will sing, words will be said, words that will hurt,
oh it's just us drifting

I was stuck there, drifting mid-impact, in the moment where my daughter's whole lifetime folded concertina-like into nothing, where she became a ghost, and perhaps I did too. My body suddenly contained life and death at the same time, like babushka dolls nestled within one another. In that eerie place, the sound of ambulance and fire engine sirens is stuck on repeat; time stretched out, to create a new reality, abruptly disjointed from our previous one.

The first time I heard sirens after being released from hospital, my body shook with sobs before I could register what was happening. The taste of nausea on my tongue, a feeling of my blood draining out through my legs, my stomach dropping sideways.

•

In the time it took for the paramedics to come, for the firefighters to bring the giant can opener to release me from the car, I breathed. I held Rima's hand until the paramedics took her, and then one of the firefighters got in her seat and held my hand. 'You're an ideal patient—very calm,' he said.

'I don't see any point in making this worse,' I replied. We didn't really need to make small talk. The others were working hard, concentrating on bending the metal without hurting my soft body. I kept my hand on my belly—*Come on, Haloumi, stay with me, little one.*

•

I was fierce about our little family; for so many years, I hadn't allowed myself to think it was possible. As a teenager, I'd stood in my school uniform at the tram stop, radiating shame as I thought about the dream

Sunday, 27 December 2009

that had woken me that morning. I'd dreamt I was struggling with a snake that grew bigger and bigger, and at the very moment I thought it would constrict me, it became a woman, and the struggle changed into something else, which made me gasp because it felt so incredibly good. *Oh no*, I said silently, solemnly, to the mannequins in the shop window. *I must be one of them.* I couldn't even say the word 'lesbian' in my head. It was a taunt, an insult hurled after all the others had been exhausted. The worst of the worst. At the school I went to, you might as well tattoo 'Bully me' on your forehead if you were going to admit to anything but vociferous heterosexuality.

I'd had boyfriends, and genuinely loved, and sometimes desired, them. That was how I could recognise the power of these feelings and responses—though they had a distinctly different social value. Having a boyfriend had won me a level of acceptance, of approval; the feeling of growing up how I was supposed to grow up. These feelings, though, threatened to mark me out, to contaminate me as abnormal, unacceptable, clearly destined for a sad, lonely, embarrassing existence. No one I knew was in a same-sex relationship—not a cousin, teacher, family friend, no one on any of the TV shows or films I'd seen. (No, that's not quite true, there was the gay lawyer in *Philadelphia*, who died.) I knew people 'like that' existed, but in a universe so shadowy and far from my own that I had no desire to go there. Yet, that morning at the tram stop, I confronted the solemn knowledge that wherever that universe was, I was already an expatriate citizen whether I liked it or not. And the fact that I was having this imaginary conversation with womanly mannequins wearing foundation garments (no racy lingerie for Camberwell shop windows, thank you!) was only further proof of my guilt.

Fast-forward several years, to university, and I was having a very different conversation, at least with a live, human woman this time.

'Have you ever been in love?' she asked.

We were making noodles (literally, not metaphorically, I'm afraid) in her room at college. This was what happened after beers and dancing if we didn't a) pass out or b) pick up boys. I preferred option c), even if I had to run the risk of a) or b) to make it a possibility.

I was carefully flippant in replying: 'Oh, I'm always in love with at least one person at any given time.'

She hopped into bed with the bowl of noodles on her lap, and patted the space next to her. I squished in and stole some noodles with my fork, acutely aware of the warmth of her leg parallel to mine on the bed.

'Really? So you're in love with someone now then? Who?'

I imagined a voice bubble that said, 'You, silly!' then carefully dismantled it and said, 'Oh, no one you know.' She pressed me further, and I came up with a boy in one of my law classes who I strongly suspected was gay. 'Anyway, he doesn't seem interested. What about you—have you ever been in love?' She said no, she didn't think so.

Before we finished the noodles, I asked, 'What would you do if your brother or sister were gay?'

'But they're not. You know them—there's no way either of them are.'

'No, but just *say*—what if one of them were?'

'But they're not, and they never would be.'

I sighed. I couldn't tell whether she was being stubborn or misunderstanding me. 'No … I mean, just imagine a hypothetical brother or sister, not J or C but another imaginary sibling, who was gay—how would you be?'

She got up and crossed the room to find her toothbrush. 'This is a stupid question—who knows how I'd be with a hypothetical imaginary sibling, anyway? I'm tired; I'm going to go to bed.'

It was a few months later, when I woke up alone and disorientated in bed after a big night out with no memory of how I'd arrived there, that I realised no amount of drinking was magically going to turn her gay, or make me brave enough to make a move. It was time for me to face up to the heartbreak, move out of college, and find a woman who might actually be interested.

The other factor, apart from my cowardice, that had prevented me from coming out was the knowledge in my gut that I wanted to have

Sunday, 27 December 2009

children. I was tortured by the thought that I had an impossible choice before me: to be true to myself, or to have the children I longed for. But other women were already challenging that impossible choice. In the Queensland Anti-Discrimination Commission, in early 1997, a lesbian couple had succeeded in challenging laws preventing them from accessing assisted reproductive services, as had several de facto couples in Victoria.[1] I walked through campus with this revolutionary information rattling around my head. Maybe I didn't have to choose. Maybe I could be with someone I loved and desired *and* have a child with them. My heart felt as if it had grown wings and was flapping through the sky a few metres ahead of me, and I smiled a big, goofy smile to myself.

•

The emergency workers surrounding me—levering the car open, cutting metal, lifting me out—were so diligent in their work, it was as though I were some ancient Etruscan vase being extracted from an archaeological dig. A screen like a photographer's reflector was fitted around the shattered windscreen so the glass didn't hit me while they prised the car open. The world folded in around me, narrowing to this small space and the faces that came into it. I held their solid arms while I was lifted, like a circus girl being passed through a hoop, letting my eyes focus on the heavy blue cotton weave of their overalls. I was strapped to the smooth plastic of a spinal board and slotted into the ambulance, a paramedic still holding my hand.

While we travelled, sirens blasting, I asked the paramedic whether he could try to find a fetal heartbeat. There was no Doppler machine in the ambulance, but he tried with a stethoscope. Things were hazy but I clearly remember the number—155 beats per minute. It confirmed what I thought I knew: Haloumi would be okay. I repeated that number to the doctors when I arrived in emergency—*155, 155*.

•

Before that little heart started beating, there was just a tiny dot—a scarcely believable little thing somewhere below my belly button. And before that, the sticky plastic cup our friend, and sperm donor, Jorge left on our dresser on a Tuesday night at the beginning of May.

'We're having ice-cream; do you want some?'

We were all a bit awkward. This was the first time we'd tried a fresh donation—all of our previous eight months' worth of attempts had been at the hospital, using his frozen samples.

'No, I'd better get on home; this isn't a social visit this time.' Jorge smiled sneakily, kissed us and left, his magazine under his arm.

•

When we arrived in emergency, I was parcelled from ambulance to examining table in a series of clicks, rolling wheels, and an efficient one-two-three. Cool surgical scissors slid under my bra straps and up my trouser legs, slicing through fabric and elastic so that my clothes fell away, creating a clear workspace—my damaged body—for the nurses and doctors who moved around me. My limbs were distant, faces moved in and out of focus. I was asked my name, my age, today's date, what had happened. I repeated these facts diligently. But, like Alice wondering 'Do cats eat bats, do bats eat cats?', I started to wonder whether I was thirty-three years old and thirty-four weeks pregnant, or thirty-four years old and thirty-three weeks pregnant.

I could hear the doctors talking over in the corner. They had wheeled the ultrasound machine in, after every man and his dog had tried to get a heartbeat with the Doppler machine, and then another Doppler with new batteries. I knew that if they'd seen a heartbeat, there would be reassurances, smiles. I was still waiting.

'Okay, so that would be the explanation …' was the only bit of the conversation I caught.

I still had my hand on my belly, now sticky with ultrasound gel. They'd had to move my hand during the scans. They did it gently, and

Sunday, 27 December 2009

I edged my fingers back each time, feeling softly for those little heels. *Come on, Haloumi, now is your moment, my beautiful one. You weren't so shy at your last ultrasound, four days ago.* I didn't want to hear an explanation, only a heartbeat.

A doctor came to me and introduced himself. He had thick white hair, a bow tie, and worst of all, a concerned look. 'I understand you've been told?'

'No, I haven't.' *Don't tell me. Don't tell me.*

But I found myself saying helpfully, 'You haven't found a heartbeat, have you?' It mustn't be easy to have to break this kind of news to women. I felt sorry for him.

'No.' There were words after that, coming out of his mouth like a speech bubble—about being induced, about labour—but I couldn't match them with any meaning.

Someone had called my mum; I could hear her voice coming from the phone held to my ear. 'We've lost our Haloumi,' I said into space.

Rima had been sent to a different hospital. Finally, I could speak to her on the phone. '*Hayet*, Haloumi didn't make it.'

I could make these words come out of my mouth; I knew I had to say them, but that doesn't mean I believed them.

Once they'd established they only had one life left to save within my body, they started rearranging the various cords and tubes attached to me, so that I could be wheeled away for a CT scan. I asked, 'Is it okay to have this scan when I'm this pregnant?'

'It's okay now,' I heard.

I was arranged like a posable doll on the narrow table, still tilted so that the full weight of my womb and baby didn't cut off the blood to my legs. My belly sloped downhill—I asked to be strapped onto the table because I felt as if I could roll off at any moment. And then, suddenly, everyone left the room, and it was me and the futuristic white donut of the scanner. The table buzzed into motion, and took me slowly in and then out again, making silent and invisible slices through my marbled flesh.

•

When I'd done the pregnancy test the first time, I'd been a bit too enthusiastic and flooded it, so that it was impossible to get any reading from the test. 'You'll just have to be patient, and wait until you need to go again,' Rima laughed. I was working from home that day, but she had to leave to catch her train.

In the nine months that we'd been trying, my period had never been this late. After that many attempts, I'd tried to discipline myself about obsessing over possible symptoms, but this time felt different. When I'd played hockey the night before, I'd gagged with nausea when I put my mouthguard in.

With the second pregnancy test, I made little rules for myself. No sitting here and staring and staring at it. I would put it on the side of the bath and come back at the designated three minutes, not a moment earlier. Within two-and-a-half minutes, I was back in the bathroom. I stared at the test and then stared at the wall. *Oh man! Wall, this looks like two lines. Two lines!* What a beautiful piece of wall was in front of my eyes, and I'd never noticed it before.

I couldn't get through to Rima, who was in a meeting. I left a hyperventilated message, and called my best mate from high school, Penny. 'I think it's positive!' She squealed, while I caveated my joy: 'I know this doesn't necessarily mean anything, I know it's early days, but it looks like it's positive. We've never had that before.'

Finally, I got Rima on the phone. '*Hayet*—I think there are two lines!'

I knew what our odds were at that early stage. We breathed out a little when my blood test came back positive; and exhaled properly a fortnight later, when we had our six-week scan, and saw a tiny, pulsing jellybean of a creature. I curled my neck up to look, and then looked at Rima. 'It looks like Yoda!' I said.

She grinned. 'Yep. And it's saying, "Pregnant, you are!"'

2
The second-best blanket

Where my memories of the immediate aftermath of the accident are acid clear, those first hours in the emergency department are morphine-clouded. Things jump from scene to scene. Suddenly, I was back from the CAT scan and my mum was washing blood from my face. 'I knew your dad would be coming soon, and he didn't need to see you like that,' she told me weeks later.

They had stapled my head wound, but it was still bleeding. 'She's lying in a pool of her own blood,' my mum said, matter-of-factly. 'Can it be re-stitched?' They re-stitched it twice before it stopped bleeding.

By the morning, my hair was bright red from the blood, and stood up in stiff curls where the blood had caked. It looked as if I'd been to some demonic hairdresser. Penny later confided that when she came to see me the next day, her first thought was that this was a bit of a funny time for me to be dyeing my hair.

I was reassured when a midwife, Jen, arrived and introduced herself. Here was something I was prepared for. 'At least I can give Haloumi a good birth,' I said. No tears had come yet. I still couldn't imagine this baby's face, alive or not. Everything was in the abstract until this child was born. I had been given a prostaglandin gel to start the induction process, but had no sense of how long it might take. While I waited, I thought of my friend Brigette.

•

Brigette was a family friend who unexpectedly fell pregnant when she was nineteen and got married. That alone was surprising enough, but then we got news that her daughter was stillborn at full term. I didn't send a card or call because I didn't know what to do. We'd always conducted our friendship in person, when we met up at the beach once or twice a year as kids and teenagers. Once we were adults, and she had moved interstate, I was unsure how to keep up the friendship and even more clueless about how to respond to her loss.

I made contact again about six years later when I was living in Sydney, and she came to visit me. She'd since had another daughter, had broken up with her husband, and was facing an acrimonious family law battle. I asked whether she sometimes wished she'd never gotten pregnant that first time. And she said, 'No. No, I'm really glad we had the time we had with Sacha—I'm glad she was my daughter.' I was surprised, because I had imagined that stillbirth was like a mathematical equation—plus one, minus one—leaving you more or less where you were before. She gave me an inkling that there was something completely unquantifiable about the loss, and the gain, which a stillborn child brought.

•

'This may be a silly question,' I said to Jen, 'but can I play the relaxation CD from our birthing course?' She nodded, and, without any fuss, my beautiful, practical sister, Erica, drove all the way across town and back to bring me the CD and CD player.

Rima and I used to joke that the key relaxation technique the birthing CDs provided was the giggle we got from hearing the hippy windchimes and the woman with a corny accent drawl out the word 'Aaaaaaffirmations'. I think of it now, and wonder that the medical staff were happy for my sister to plug the CD player into sockets used for lifesaving equipment, and to let the softly spoken platitudes of hypno-birthing wash across the hard surfaces of the emergency room. People humour you when death is this close by.

And, somehow, the affirmations worked. Somehow, I unzipped myself from the hospital drama scene, from all the tubes, monitors and bandages, and I was back, floating in the Coogee sea baths, cupping light-filled water softly in my hands, the salt water and sunlight washing against my belly. Haloumi was big then—it was only a week or so before we left Sydney. I remember thinking at the time, 'I need to hold onto this; this will be my good place to come back to when I'm in labour.' Not complicated, not difficult, just light so bright I could close my eyes and still feel it all around me, as though it were the water I floated in.

•

I first discovered the Coogee baths when I was staying in Sydney for an internship; before I had graduated, before I had torn away from Melbourne. Even then, I ached for a baby. That was the whole point of the internship—to get a graduate-lawyer position, so I could save up for a baby and, hopefully, find a partner in the process. I had ducked under the water and surfaced with new knowledge: that I would swim here pregnant. That knowledge latched tightly somewhere in my belly, pulling me towards Sydney and back onto that plane. I'd felt so vindicated when it came true, when I immersed my rounded body in the same salt water and felt a beautiful squirming that was not my own—a small swimming body within my own swimming body. It was an odd sense of infinity, of being one small bit of this Mandelbrot universe—a pattern within a pattern, with another, smaller, pattern inside.

•

The calm of the impact was still there, but now everything really hurt, especially my hardened womb. Jen was trying to monitor my contractions, which were lasting over six minutes each.

After the CT scan, and after the possibility of spinal injury was ruled out, they released me from the neck brace, which had been starting to feel like a sarcophagus. I immediately wanted to turn over, to rest on all fours, and my mum and the midwife started to help me, but I quickly realised that my body wasn't responding the way it used to. I couldn't move smoothly into the yoga poses I had practised every day, and that I had hoped would help me deliver this baby. My body was heavy, tight with quickly appearing bruises, and when I tried to bend my bandaged left knee, there was a queasy pain. I managed to sit on the edge of the bed and swing my legs down, but was afraid of collapsing forwards. Gently, Mum lifted my arms, with their vines of tubes and monitors, and ducked under them, so that I could hug her and melt into her shoulder.

I was so thirsty. I kept asking for water, but all I was allowed was chunks of ice from a polystyrene cup. I would roll the ice in my mouth, choke slightly, spit it out; or, if I was feeling particularly gutsy, crunch it into many small icebergs. Erica held the cup for me, quietly and calmly. This was a pain I needed to hold in my gaze, with my full concentration. I wanted to deliver this child, to see him or her for myself, before accepting any bad news from a fuzzy ultrasound machine. This pain would get me there.

'Hannah.' We'd been relatively unprodded for an uncountable number of hours, while I crunched ice and worked my way, hand over hand, through the pain. It was the obstetrician, back again. 'We'd like to do an internal examination again and check your progress.'

I was startled. 'The midwife did one not so long ago and she thought I was at about 3 centimetres.'

'I know, but we need to do another one, to see how things are going.'

It hurt, and he wasn't impressed with my progress.

'The problem is, with all your other injuries, this needs to happen pretty quickly. I think we're going to need to do a caesar.'

The second-best blanket

•

'The problem,' the obstetrician explained six weeks later, 'was that we were concerned about you going into a state called DIC—disseminated intravascular coagulopathy. It's when you've got a big bleed—like the placental abruption—which pulls in all the clotting agents in your blood, so that the rest of your blood loses its ability to clot.'

'Which is a bad thing,' I added helpfully.

'Yes, particularly when you have other wounds. No matter how much blood we transfuse in, you can still bleed to death. We were testing your clotting factors to monitor you for DIC, and by about 3 a.m. they were starting to fall, which meant you were starting to go into DIC. Those six-minute contractions were probably not contractions. It's more likely that they were an indication of Couvelaire uterus—bleeding into the wall of the uterus. If I was dealing with your case again, I would send you straight for a C-section.'

•

Suddenly, I was being prepped for surgery.

'This is very unlikely, but there's a possibility that we may need to do a hysterectomy.'

He saw my face, and moved from disclosure into reassurance mode.

'We'll try to do a lower-section caesarean, but if we have concerns about the liver and spleen bleeding, we may need to embolise them, and that would require a bigger incision. At this stage, we're hoping we can conservatively manage the liver and spleen bleeding, and not operate on them.'

'I only have one kidney,' I announced to the obstetrician. I'm sure I'd already told that to someone in the emergency room, but I wanted to make sure he knew now, so that he didn't just have to guess from my silent, scarred body.

'Why was your kidney removed?' He was genuinely interested. This was nice, but also a little bit worrying.

'I had an ectopic ureter, so I kept getting recurrent kidney infections. I had surgery here,' I reached around my still-big belly and touched a thin scar just above my pubic bone, 'to fix where the ureter went into my bladder, and then they went to remove the damaged bit of my kidney.' I touched my side, where a thick scar ran below my ribs. 'But when they operated on my kidney, they accidentally hit an artery that wasn't supposed to be there, and I lost a lot of blood. So they just took the whole kidney, and closed me up and did a blood transfusion.'

'When was this?'

'In 1983. I was seven.'

What I didn't say was *Please be careful operating on me.*

Before they wheeled me into theatre, Jen asked if we wanted to pick an outfit and blanket for the baby. It still seemed very unreal. My sister had brought in a bag full of baby things that my mum had made or bought for Haloumi. My hand hovered between two blankets Mum had knitted. One was just too lovely to be cremated—I wanted to save it for a living baby (callously, I think now)—so I picked the other one.

•

There was no night on Sunday, 27 December. When I closed my eyes from the general anaesthetic, it felt as if only a moment had passed before I was opening them again; but this time, the weight and pain of my pregnant womb were gone. My fingers crept to my side—my belly felt soft, flat, bandaged. For a second I felt relief, and then remembered why I felt so much lighter. A face moved into my field of vision and came close enough to be less blurry. It was Jen. She handed me a photo. 'You had a little girl.'

Everything else faded into background and all I could see was her—our daughter—with her round cheeks, dark hair and a pointy little Rima-chin. Our daughter, wrapped in the second-best blanket, which instantly became the best, most beautiful blanket for being wrapped around her. I couldn't be stingy with my love now that she was born; I couldn't hold off on loving my child because she was no longer alive.

3

Shavasana

We had one day with our baby daughter—Monday, 28 December. One day to name her, to give her a bath, to hold her and sniff her head and memorise every millimetre of her. People asked me questions while she was in my arms, but their voices sounded distant; I couldn't look away from her face. She had a tiny bruise on her right eyebrow, lots of dark hair, big chubby cheeks, a serious, expressive mouth. I could imagine teenage attitude coming out of that mouth. I unfurled her little fist. A small, strong hand.

Before I had my own dead baby, I couldn't imagine anything more macabre than a dead child. A dead baby was a plot device, pure metaphor, something frightening precisely because it was so unthinkable. But my dead baby, you would have loved her! On any objective scale, she was clearly the most beautiful baby girl ever born. She had a world-weary, uber-cool way about her. Not for her the corporeal indignities of living, screaming, pooing babies. Here she was, the mysterious one who'd been kicking me all along, now terminally mysterious and unknowable, yet so specifically herself. Birth is the 'big reveal' of motherhood, when a hypothetical, potentially generic baby becomes your own child. And yes, my heart split forever, with her part of it not setting off to walk around outside my body but heading for a stupidly small coffin and a private cremation.

My brother, Jeremy, arrived just as I was being prepared to be sent from ICU for another CT scan to check on the internal bleeding. He brought with him the soft grey rabbit he and his fiancée had given us for our baby at Christmas. I entrusted both rabbit and baby to my mum and the midwives, as the orderlies wheeled my bed out the door and towards the lifts. Jeremy took my hand, and stayed with me all the way down to the scanner. He is known for being the least chatty in a family of extreme chattiness. But there was nothing awkward about being quiet with him. I was reluctant to relinquish his hand when I was moved onto the bed of the scanner, but knowing he was there, solid and waiting for me as the machinery sent me into the tunnel of the CT scanner and out again, enabled me to breathe quietly. When I emerged, I took his hand again for the journey back to ICU—my new alien, but life-sustaining, universe.

•

On Christmas night, I'd driven to the airport with my sister and mum to pick up Jeremy. He was back from Germany because he'd been offered some lucrative rigging contracts. His German fiancée was having knee surgery and rehabilitation, but would soon follow him to Australia. We were staying at my dad and stepmum's house over Christmas, before we moved into our new house after relocating from Sydney. I had missed my family so much in my seven years living in Sydney, and now it felt like things were gathering in again. We'd farewelled Jez early on Boxing Day morning when he caught a lift with a friend, heading down to work at the Falls Festival on the coast. He had hugged me, then ducked down to give my belly a quick peck. 'See ya, Haloumi.'

•

'Have you named her yet?' more than one person asked me. I know they were being kind, but the question and being hurried irritated me. I couldn't name her without Rima being there and, despite my pleading for her to be transferred, she was still in another hospital, being treated for broken ribs and a broken hand, and awaiting release.

'Haloumi' had worked well as our nickname for a growing, kicking bump, but the quiet baby girl in my arms needed a real name. We couldn't keep referring to her as a type of cheese. In the busy weeks before the accident, in our preparations for Christmas and the move to Melbourne, Rima and I had chewed over the topic of baby names many times. We were settled on a boy's name, but girls' names were more difficult. We wanted an Arabic name, a connection to Rima's Lebanese heritage, but so many of the names I loved provoked the response from Rima, 'Oh, *that*? That's an old lady's name! We can't call Haloumi that!'

At last, Rima appeared at the door of my ICU room, wearing her brother's tracksuit pants and a hospital gown, her broken hand in a sling. She had discharged herself from the Alfred. I was holding our still-unnamed baby in my arms. 'Rima, come meet your daughter,' I said. 'She looks like you, *hayet*—look at her chin.' So much had happened since the ambulance officer had prised her hand out of mine so that he could remove her from the wreckage. All our haggling over baby names was irrelevant—here was our daughter and she needed us to name her.

Zainab was the first name that tumbled out of my mouth when I asked Rima what we should name her. It was one of the old-lady names we'd argued about, but now Rima said, 'Yes, Zainab,' without taking her eyes off our baby's face. And I thought of our friend Izzy, the way she would squeeze us and say, '*Kha-li-la*!' (my darling) like a Lebanese *tayta* (grandmother). It felt strange to declare her name, when she would never get to use it herself. But there she was, our Zainab Khalila. It was a big name for a small person, and particularly for one we knew so little about; so, often I would shorten it and think of her as little Z.

•

Shavasana. It's a fancy yoga word for lying on the floor. It's also called 'corpse pose', because imagining yourself as a corpse is a good way to relax every muscle in the body. When I started going to yoga classes a month or so after being released from hospital, the yoga teacher would introduce shavasana, and the tears would run sideways across my cheeks and make wet patches on the yoga mat near each of my ears. I would lie there, slack faced, heavy limbed, and think of little Z, her face soft with the absolute calm of death. Before our accident, I'd been safely insulated from death. It was something that mostly happened to old people, and corpses were horror-movie props.

Now, on the yoga mat, I would test out what it felt like to be dead, not in a melodramatic or suicidal way, but because it was so odd to be alive when I could feel so little continuity between my life 'before' and 'after'. It was hard to shake the thought that maybe, somehow, I had in fact died in the accident, that maybe I was a ghost. Death had found its way into my body, had carried off its victim under my very ribs, yet here I was, fraudulently breathing in and out. I was so alien to myself that I wondered if the old Hannah had died, and a new one had been born, like Venus, as a naked adult woman, appearing not on a shell from the ocean, but on an emergency-room trolley, the doctors and nurses around me like the four winds.

•

When I'd first held Zainab, she'd been warm. After Rima had come, after we'd bathed her, marvelled at her toes, dressed her in a small suit with brightly coloured stripes, I held her again and she was noticeably colder. *We don't have much time, little one*, I thought. Did we put a nappy on her? It is a silly, small detail, but it bothers me that I can't remember. The suit was soft, soft cotton and had little giraffe faces on the feet. At one stage, one of the midwives or social workers brought in a tiny pink dress with lace and bows—exactly the kind of thing we would never have picked for her. 'Would this fit?'

We politely declined, but once the woman left, I was disparaging: 'She may be dead, but we're not dressing her in *that*.' And we laughed the brittle laughter of the bereaved. I realised afterwards that it had probably been donated by a family who knew this feeling first hand, and I felt unaccountably mean for mocking their kind gift. Zainab, though, looked solemn; *Nope, she wasn't going to wear that, thanks!* We felt wicked as we laughed. Guilty for allowing our faces to crack wide with laughter, disloyal for producing anything but tears. Still, it was a release—an emptying-out of the dark waters of grief, like weeping out loud together but without the fear that our sadness co-mingled would drown us.

Sometime after Rima got there, Jackie and Jazzie arrived. They had been discharged from the Children's Hospital—Jazzie with a fractured hip, and a suspected fracture in her wrist; Jackie with a badly broken nose, stitches in her lip and mild concussion. Jackie had been sitting in the middle row of seats in our Nimbus, designed to fold down to give access to the third row of seats. In the impact, the seat had malfunctioned and folded, tilting her forwards, so that her face hit the back of my seat, or her own knees; we don't know which. The ambulance had taken them to the Children's Hospital as unaccompanied minors, while Rima and I had been sent to different hospitals. (Though, thanks to an extraordinary coincidence, the one and only person they knew who was employed at the Children's Hospital—Charlie, a longstanding family friend—was on duty in the ER and ended up caring for them.) My stepmum, Debbie, got there as quickly as she could, and stayed with them all night. A week later, Jasmin presented me with a drawing she had done with her left hand (her right was in a cast) of her and Jackie in hospital beds, tears running down their faces, Debbie on a camp bed between them.

When they arrived in my ICU room, they were wearing blue scrubs from the Children's Hospital, as their clothes had been cut off too.

Jazzie was in a wheelchair; Jackie's face was swollen from the impact, with surgical tape and gauze on her cut lip and broken nose. They had come to meet their baby sister. And to reunite us as the human contents of TAZ 012, together once more after being splintered apart across three different hospitals.

Here is our family portrait—me holding Zainab in the centre, Rima leaning in on one side, and Jazzie and Jackie leaning in on the other. Our faces were shiny with tears, swollen with bruises. My hair was a mass of blood-red Medusa coils. I was too bereft to remember to close my mouth or even to look properly at the camera, and Rima was unsure whether she was supposed to try to smile. Jazzie's eyebrows were incredulous; *Is this really happening?* (This is not how she thought she'd meet her baby sister.) But Jackie's gaze was level, direct, reproachful—not vindictive, but heavy with truth. *This. This is what happened.* I want the person who caused our accident to experience that gaze. Or, really, for every driver to see it as they lay their hands on a steering wheel.

Jazzie, then Jackie, cradled their little sister in their arms. It was difficult with a broken arm. We took a photo of Zainab surrounded by our clasped hands. Her lips had gone a dark red, as though she were wearing lipstick for newborns. 'It's the delicate skin on her lips drying out,' a nurse explained. It meant she was looking less 'sleeping newborn' and more 'funeral photo'. I loved her still, but I was glad we'd got some photos early on.

I am not religious, but in Rima's faith, it was important to hold a funeral as quickly as possible. We planned something small. When Penny and I were in Year Nine at high school, Penny had confided in me that her mother, a hospital chaplain, often had to plan funerals for babies. As teenagers, we treated this as a weird horror-movie fact, remarkable mainly for the reaction it could elicit. I hadn't considered what it felt like for the parents of those babies. I asked my dad to contact Penny and her mum, Judith, to ask for their help. I imagine it is very hard to write a eulogy for a baby who has died before she is born, but Judith did that for us.

Penny came and sat vigil in my ICU room. It was her hands, along with my mother's and my sister's, that helped Rima and me give Zainab her first and last bath. ICU only allowed immediate family to visit, so we told them she was my sister—and, in a way, it was true.

We had been inseparable as thirteen year olds, writing long notes to one another in class, borrowing lines and characters from our favourite movies, songs and books. We'd later stolen one another's boyfriends and become estranged twice, but each time we reconnected through writing letters; a sorority in words that built a shared history bigger than any betrayal. In Year Ten, after I'd written something particularly angsty, my English teacher suggested I read *Cat's Eye* by Margaret Atwood. 'It's one of the Year Twelve texts,' she explained, 'but I think you'll like it.' Somehow, it became a book whose storyline will always be entangled with my high school years, when both Penny and I read and re-read it, and with our friendship. Like Elaine and Cordelia in *Cat's Eye*, Penny and I had lost each other for a while, but, unlike them, we found one another again and were kinder to one another than we had been as teenagers.

That night, Rima slept on two chairs pushed together next to my ICU bed. The next morning, she and my dad sat on the bed and I dictated a death notice for the paper. No one argued about the wording. I wondered aloud whether it should go in the 'births' or 'deaths' column, or both. Strictly, it was a double bill, and I wanted her birth *and* death acknowledged, but I conceded when Dad said the funeral home would probably just put it in the 'deaths' column.

To prepare for the funeral that afternoon, the ICU nurses tilted my bed so that my head was lowered, and washed the blood from my hair. Warm rivulets ran up my scalp, as though I were showering upside down. The nurses washed gently around the wound on the right side of my head. They rinsed all that bloody water from my hair and rinsed it again, then blow-dried it; not the way a hairdresser does, but the way you do getting ready for work in the morning. It wasn't styled, but it was better than the Medusa coils.

My sister had been to see our car in the wrecker's yard and to collect our belongings from it. There, folded neatly on the dashboard, were my glasses. In the chaos of the emergency department and the fog of the morphine, I hadn't even realised they were missing. I was relieved to discover that the closed-in focus wasn't just my shell-shocked brain but also my own ordinary short-sightedness. I was also reunited with my handbag—such an ordinary object, but it was something from before, and its familiarity made our new circumstances feel all the more alien. I opened my little mirrored compact to put on some make-up, fuzzily remembering my routine, usually undertaken on the train to Newcastle. First, the silvery grey eyeshadow along the lid line, then getting lighter from the outer corner. Then the pearly cream on the inner hollow and under the brow. Finally, a lip gloss. The mirror only afforded a view of small slots of my face, which was just as well.

For the first time since they had cut my clothes off me in emergency, I wore clothes rather than hospital linen. Rima had brought in the nightie the girls had given me for Christmas—soft cotton, with pink and green florals, and (as requested) buttons at the front that would be practical for breastfeeding a new baby. Perhaps a bit more nanna than my usual style, but beautiful because the girls had chosen it for me. Still, nighties weren't quite funeral attire, even in these circumstances, so I needed something else over the top of it. My sister brought in a black top of hers and we stretched it gingerly over my head, cutting the waistband with scissors to get it over my post-partum belly.

I was to be transferred into a wheelchair with my broken leg raised in front of me. There was a moment of consternation when we realised the leg board I would sit on and that would support my broken left knee, held straight in a splint, was designed to support a right leg. A nurse was about to take it back and change it over, when we all realised, sheepishly, that it was the same on both sides; we just needed to flip it over and it could support a left leg.

A new ICU nurse—a young woman, Janelle, with a long, dark plait down her back—began her shift just as we were heading downstairs for

Z's funeral. She was a watchful guest, sitting in the last row of seats. Our other guest at the funeral was the Le Pine woman, who was going to take our daughter to be cremated. She waited patiently after the short service while we said our goodbyes. Being in the wheelchair, I couldn't lean over to kiss Zainab, so I pulled the whole casket onto my lap and kissed her cool cheek, already wet with our tears. 'This will have to do,' I thought. This will have to suffice for all the child-care drop-offs, the first day at school, have-fun-at-camp goodbyes, airport-departure-lounge hugs—so many smaller farewells exchanged for this big one. 'Please take care of her,' I said to the Le Pine woman, and she squeezed my hand.

Afterwards, we sat in the hospital cafeteria. Numb. I drank real coffee, I chewed through a significant piece of cake, without tasting either. My sister came back to the table, and laid a black-and-white notebook in front of me with a pen. 'Write,' she said. 'It's what you do.'

4

The torture booties

That second night in ICU, it was just me, the ICU nurse and the torture booties. Rima had gone home at my insistence; her ribs were hurting her, and another night sleeping on chairs wasn't going to help. The torture booties were a clever invention designed to prevent me from dying of a blood clot, as I wasn't able to take anti-clotting medications due to the internal bleeding. They were strapped to my feet and legs, and inflated and deflated on a timer providing 'intermittent pneumatic compression'. What it really felt like was a robust whack to the soles of my feet every four minutes or so. Four minutes seemed to be just enough time for me to start drifting off to sleep before—*whack, whack*—they went off again, and I jerked my broken knee, so that the staples pulled and the bone ached.

The new notebook from Erica was out of reach, but by the red glow of the heartbeat monitor on my finger, I rummaged in my handbag on the nightstand and found my old yellow notebook.

•

I had bought the yellow notebook on the Newcastle campus the week I'd got the phone call telling me my pregnancy blood test had come

The torture booties

back positive. The nurse had been deliciously deadpan. 'Yep, it's all fine.' I had to prod her to get the exact level (of hCG or human chorionic gonadotropin, the pregnancy hormone, in my blood) and then for reassurance that the test was positive. I felt like Alice in Wonderland after she ate the mushroom, putting her hand on her head to work out whether she is shrinking or growing. My body was out of whack, unpredictable in a way it hadn't been since I was a teenager. I had been waking up in the early hours of each night since we'd begun to have real suspicions that this might be it—at first I thought it was nerves and over-excitement. But incessant googling also told me that the surging progesterone of early pregnancy tends to make you tired during the day and interrupt your sleep at night, so maybe that was playing a role.

I found an image of Leonardo Da Vinci's Annunciation on the internet, and added small speech bubbles:

Archangel Gabriel: 'You've got a hCG level of 2063!'
Mary: 'So, does that mean a yes or a no?'

•

With cannula-punctured hands I opened the yellow notebook carefully, holding in all the pieces of paper documenting this pregnancy: ultrasound results, blood tests, brochures for prenatal yoga. I opened it to a new page, after my notes from our birthing class, and started to write.

Tuesday, 29 December 2009

I look like heavily discounted supermarket stock—sticky from all the previous price stickers, and leaking in unexpected places. In ICU, they don't bother with the neat little patient ID plastic bangles—they stick your barcode ID directly onto your skin, securing it with a clear plastic dressing, like a piece of clingwrapped ham. My limbs feel foreign to me. My arms are bandaged and puffy with bruises, I'm only just reclaiming them for my own use. My legs I haven't quite remembered yet. They belong in the land below sheets. Somehow, I feel like I've just been born—uncertain of the sensations assaulting me and reliant on others for my basic needs. I am tentative about my body. It doesn't feel quite mine again yet. Indeed I'm not really sure whether I haven't been completely reborn with a new body that I will have to learn how to use again from the beginning.

I dreamt that the sun was rising as the pieces of a shipwreck floated into a beachy shore, the water sparkling innocently where only the night before it had been a violent breaker of things and bodies. Uneven chunks of wood were gently tipped over and over along the sand by foamy waves. The sea isn't malicious—it is just the sea and the weather is just the weather. It would be pointless to expect fairness.

I woke again with the *whack* of the torture booties, and all that salt water spilled over into sobs—for my sore knee, for my tiredness, for my baby girl. Janelle, my ICU nurse, came, apologising that she couldn't turn the boots off without doctor's orders. She dragged over a stool so she could sit by the bed, took my hand in hers and asked me about the accident. I told her my opiate-smudged story, and wept while she leaned her head against the bed and listened, until I couldn't cry anymore and we both dozed off, only to wake again with a start when the torture booties went off.

When I woke up next, it felt like a proper awakening, one where a decent chunk of sleep had happened in the interim. It was nearly morning, and the new nurse was muttering to herself about faulty equipment and what the doctors would do if they saw that the compression booties had somehow been turned off in the middle of the night.

5
The crazy lady in ward four

The day after Zainab's funeral, I was transferred to the trauma ward. I was wheeled—bed and all—out of ICU, past unmoving patients attached to life support machines or breathing apparatus, past their worried relatives. I was being returned to the land of the living, but frail, bruised and dependent on others for everything. I had my first shower, I took my first steps (with the help of the hospital physio and a Zimmer frame), I ate my first hospital meal. Everything was new to me, everything felt different. I joked that instead of having a baby, I had become a baby. I had anticipated night wakings, changing nappies, first steps—just not my own. But here I was, being the helpless one needing assistance to move, to go to the toilet, to wash, to eat.

My life took on the pace of hospital routines. Big Tony came at 7 a.m., with a clean jug of iced water and a clean glass. He would take away the rubbish, and carefully attach a new bin liner to my hospital table with a bulldog clip. He moved quietly, trying not to wake me if I was sleeping. If I was awake, he was the first day-staff person I would see—a welcome reminder that the long, stretching night was over, that breakfast was coming and, soon after that, Rima, Mum, Dad or Penny. We made light of the hospital meals. When I grumbled over a rubbery croissant, Mum disappeared into the bathroom, and reappeared with a kooky grin and the hospital hair-dryer in hand. She plugged it in, and crisped the pastry up nicely.

In the evening, it was Little Tony bringing a new jug of iced water—sunset, in the hospital universe. He had similar hair and features to Big Tony but was as short and thin as Big Tony was big and wide. I wondered whether they were related.

I had a room to myself, with a bathroom, but there was nonetheless a curtain between my bed and the glass-panelled door. People would dance attendance behind the curtain, tweak it back with a finger, stick their heads around it to comical effect. When I needed to get to the bathroom, I would banish visitors behind it; things worked better without an audience.

During the day, the social worker came to see me with the Transport Accident Commission paperwork. She took me through the claim form, and I was surprised to find injuries listed that I hadn't known I had. The next time the doctors did their rounds, I asked about these extra injuries and discovered that some were incorrect (no fractured vault of skull, hooray) but some were correct. I had thought the ache in my breast was my heart breaking, but it turned out it was my fractured sternum.

The physio came to teach me how to go up and down stairs on crutches. We put her off for a day. When she came back, I was still weary. 'There are some steps at the end of the hall. We can practise there,' she said, enthusiastic and way, way too healthy looking. I shook my head. I was still not prepared to acknowledge the existence of the other end of the hall. The thought of stepping outside my own room made me swallow with fear. Resolute, she came back with a wooden step, so I could practise right outside my room. She helped me past the curtain and out the door, where lino-floored corridor stretched into the distance. I focused on my legs, which were sticking out from the bottom of my nightie, the left clothed in a red and black velcro splint, and both puffy with ripening bruises.

'Okay; so, when you're going up a step, you need to start with your good leg, then the bad leg, then the crutches.' We did a few steps, before I couldn't help but object.

'This leg isn't bad—it's just injured. And my "good" leg is sore too. Can we call them something else?'

'Um, okay. I guess so. What are you going to call them?'

I breathed in. 'This one is Alfred, and this one is Hillary.'

'Okay,' she smiled. 'So, when you go up a step, start with Hillary, then Alfred, then the crutches.'

'Okay.'

Despite my protests, the physios also took my Zimmer frame away. Where the frame had hovered helpfully, I would now lean two crutches against the bed, or try to balance them in the gap between bed and nightstand. In the night I woke and fumbled for the crutches, knocking first one then the other to the floor. I tried to reach for them but I was stuck, and had to press the assistance buzzer. The night nurse came and, after helping me to the bathroom and back to bed, disappeared with a conspiratorial look, reappearing shortly with my beloved Zimmer frame.

Other family and friends started coming to visit. My uncle and aunt sat on the end of my bed, and squeezed my hand while we had a good chat about nighties. My midwife, Jen, visited, and brought me home-made rhubarb and strawberry cheesecake. I wolfed it down, while we talked about *Where the Wild Things Are*. Matt, Steve, Sam and Sal all came in at once. Matt hugged me first and surprised me by sobbing into my neck. It was a relief. It meant I could sob too; I could bring out these pictures of our still, little daughter, invite old friends in to the weep-fest that had become my life. I had words I could say when people looked at these pictures. 'My hair was red and curly from all the blood. I look like another person. At least I know that red's not my colour.' *Ha ha*. I laughed—sometimes it helped. But it came out unnaturally, like an actor pronouncing the words, 'Ha ha ha'—high and voice-like. After a while, I worked out why and added the explanation to my hilarious repertoire: 'I can't laugh properly because my belly hurts from the caesar and my chest hurts from my broken sternum, so I just have to laugh in my mouth—ha ha ha.'

They had never seen me like this. *I* had never seen me like this. I was a stranger to myself—a wounded, maddened woman in a hospital bed.

Tash, an old school friend, called. The last time we'd spoken, it was so I could get her recommendations for maternity hospitals. She'd just had her third baby, and I had been looking forward to being in Melbourne and on maternity leave at the same time as she was. Tash had lost a little brother before I met her, at the start of high school, and in Year Seven she had been hit by a car while getting off a tram. Now this knowledge meant something very different to me; like text that had suddenly become legible. 'There is no silver lining,' she said. 'Don't let anyone tell you "everything happens for a reason"—there is no upside to a child dying.'

As long as visitors were around, I could keep it together. Rima filled in the pink meal order form for me each day, and when dinner arrived, we would lift off the heavy plastic covers with great ceremony, announcing steamed fish and salad, or vegetable omelette. As eight o'clock neared, the ward got quieter, and I would kiss Rima goodbye and watch her disappear behind the curtain, listening for the sound of the door closing.

One night, a baby started crying in the corridor. My visitors all gone for the day, I sobbed along silently. *Oh, my little love, it's hard, I know.* It was an unfamiliar noise to me, that little cry, little eh-eh-eh sobs from a small, shaking chest. I wondered, 'What would Zainab have sounded like in full voice? Where was she?' I wanted to hear my child's voice, I wanted to hear her cry. But I also thought, 'Wherever she is, she must be so scared.' Crying that kitten cry with no one to hear her, to offer a breast, their arms, a heartbeat. I shook when I realised that she lost my heartbeat at exactly the time I lost hers, but while her heartbeat had been a novelty to me, mine had been her constant companion, from her very first stirrings as a few little cells. *Oh, my little one, it's okay, little one,* I hushed that little stranger-baby in the hallway, from my bed, as well as my own sobbing self. I'd lost my moving, mysterious bump, as well as the still, little baby she'd become, so that it felt like an amputation as much as a bereavement—a piece of me severed and lost forever, leaving a gap that no amount of tears could fill.

My body still didn't remember the distinctions between nighttime and daytime, and while it felt tired, I still woke every few hours. There's no such thing as real darkness in a hospital ward. In the bluish glow, I found the button for the light, on the bed-goes-up-bed-goes-down controller, and opened my black-and-white notebook.

Wednesday, 30 December 2009

Now that I've started writing, suddenly it is hard to stop. Words soak out of me like blood. They spot my skin like measles and appear like a coating on my tongue. They leak out of every orifice, soaking into notebooks like the blood that haemorrhaged from my organs. I'm certainly talking too much but I always did that. This is different. Things are so heavy with meaning—there is so much I need to get across.

My trouble now is getting time to eat and sleep because I want to write so much. It used to be so hard to get the words out. Now, it is as though the impact crushed me like a blueberry and all these words came flowing out in dark staining lines of juice.

My handwriting was a fourteen year old's again, punctuated with love hearts and sad faces with lines of small teardrops. The black-and-white notebook became my journal while the yellow book filled with lists—names of every caregiver I encountered, movies I wanted to watch, books I needed to read, questions for the doctor, things I wanted my mum to buy on her shopping expeditions for me. 'Hannah's Rules for Hospital'. Suddenly life felt so short—there were so many things that I needed to do *right now*. Odd memories came back to me: the old ivory bangle of Mum's that I used to sniff as a four year old—where was it? My dad obligingly found it and brought it in. Thirty years later it still had the same comforting smell, and I wore it day and night. I collected other talismans to have around me—Zainab's blankets, knitted by Mum and Penny, and the soft grey bunny my brother and his fiancée had given us.

With Zainab's funeral over, her death (and birth) notice published and our sad news trickling out to friends, family and the world, I filled the long hospital days, and longer nights, with lists and projects: arranging my return to work, planning the garden at our new house, requesting pen refills, contacting my high school art teacher, negotiating relations between Rima and my family. 'You realise, don't you,' my psychologist remarked months later, 'that when you first called me from the trauma unit, you were quite manic.'

Thursday, 31 December 2009

It is so easy to get tricked into thinking that time is some substance that comes in measurable, equivalent units. As though we can compare surviving the last two days with surviving the next two days—as if your chances are as good. Instead every moment in time is its own catastrophe—its own miracle. A sibling to the moment which came before it, with its own personality, its own idiosyncracies and significance. Maybe it will be an average Joe Citizen moment, significant only to its loved ones—maybe it will be an Adolf Hitler moment.

If I could take my tiny sewing scissors and cut carefully around that moment—just cut along my line of sight when I saw the four-wheel drive swinging onto my side of the road. Just snip away that moment of impact, cut along to the quiet bit, where suddenly we were still, just before Rima started screaming. We'll lift that piece carefully out of the picture and put it down somewhere else. And then we'll pull those little edges together and stitch them, leaving a little more room around my legs and belly. Some blood noses and bruises we can deal with, but let's just skip that bone-breaking,

The crazy lady in ward four

placenta-abrupting, heart-stopping moment of impact. I'm happy even to bargain over a broken patella.

But when I lift my scissors and try to pluck that offending moment with my finger and thumb, it is all attached. It's that dilemma when you want to cut a picture from a magazine and on the back is the other picture you want to keep—terrible choices! So I find I can't cut out that nasty little moment of impact without cutting everything else. There are no neat edges.

Even if I could do the fine snipping and stitching, I still can't breathe life into my monster-moment. Because even if I wish for it without that ugly impact moment, I'd still be disfiguring time— amputating a moment, which, for someone else, might be the shining star of their lives. Time is not mine to snip.

Enough of the philosophising. My mission for today is to eat protein. Sharon, my nurse here in the trauma ward, is worried about my albumin levels and I can't just blame it on the hospital food. I'm thinking this might be a good excuse to ask Rima and Erica to revisit the Afghan chicken shop on Sydney Road up near Pentridge and bring me back some bbq chicken goodness.

And there shall be a festival of eggs. I think of the wallchart in Mrs Galt's home economics kitchen classroom—showing the egg in cross-section, yellow yolk suspended on its twisted umbilical-like cord with a neat arrow, 'Albumin'. Perhaps that is what I need—an explanatory diagram?

One of my windows is starting to go a light aqua blue—a relief to have morning draw a bit nearer with promised distraction and food.

For New Year's Eve, and with special permission from the doctors, Rima brought in a bottle of Bollinger, and, with my mum, cracked it open and tried to convince the nurses to have some with us. We cackled hysterically about Alfred and Hillary, bedpans and pain meds. 'You're asking the nurses for Endor,' said Rima. 'I don't think that's actually what it's called. Endor is the Ewok's home planet in *Star Wars*!'

We phoned the girls. My dad was being super protective and wanted them to go to bed at ten, but it was New Year's Eve, after all, and we insisted that he let them stay up for the countdown. In the early hours of 2010, the champagne clearing from my head, I wrote an earnest letter to the new year.

Friday, 1 January 2010

Dear 2010,
Oh I had thought you would be so different already, and I haven't even seen two hours of you yet. But I promised my Haloumi that I would be open to surprises. Please let that include some happy surprises as well as the rough and unfunny one 2009 dealt us.

My hopes are too delicate and frankly I'm too scared to hope or wish for anything at the moment. But I can start with what I've got and from where I am now. Right now I have my beautiful Rima and our beautiful girls. Please don't go hurting them just yet, 2010?

During the day, I could hold onto the raft of family and friends and the distractions of food, doctors' rounds and the physio or social worker. Nighttime was harder—it was just me and the big salty sorrow, with the beam of light from the night nurse swinging around slowly every so often. Pauline, the night nurse who had returned my Zimmer frame, often heard me weeping and came in to see if I was okay. She would pull up a chair and we would talk. One night, to try to calm me, she offered to rub my back. I rolled onto my tummy and with the fancy-smelling oil I had bought to rub into my stretch marks, she laid her hands on me and smoothed out some of my sadness, so that I could sleep for a little while.

Tuesday, 5 January 2010 1.10 a.m.

I don't understand with all the buckets I am crying how I can also be peeing so much. There must be some great inland sea inside me. Perhaps when I move around you can hear me sloshing?

The crazy lady in ward four

Oh I am in so much pain right now—a choir of pain, from the deep baritone ache of my knee to the sharp peaks of breathing with this broken chest bone. And over the top comes a weird melody of moans which I have never heard myself make before—a keening series of wavering 'ahhs' and alto 'ohs'. I remember reading Shakespeare plays in high school and laughing with Penny at all the 'Ah me!' and 'Alas!' exclamations. But that was the luxuriously naïve laughter of someone who had not felt sorrow so visceral that it makes you cry out in pain.

And please don't think that my analgesic needs are being neglected! Pauline and Pervin have just brought me my strong pain meds—signing them off in tandem as though I were a library book. No, I am being looked after well in that department—yet not too much, so I'm not living in a morphine fug.

No, while some of the other singers in this choir sing on the frequency of physical pain, most of them specialise in the other end of the spectrum—in sadness and madness. These are my two torture masters. They would quite like to drive me to a bad place of hurt and hate. They are taking me somewhere whether I like it or not, but I am pushing for a gentler destination—a silly puerile comic-grotesque direction in which people name their own legs. I know Alfred (left) and Hillary (right) are a bit old fashioned, but I really didn't get a lot of time to think about it. One must make snap decisions sometimes and live with those decisions.

I need to find a type of crazy in which you can laugh at the most humiliating and revolting things, because this is the reality of my life right now—stinking out the room with farts that make even the flowers weep.

6
Frida and me

By day five, they wanted to send me home.

'I have patients recovering from exactly the same knee surgery on the orthopaedic wards who are home already by day four,' said the nurse manager.

I stared at her for a second. I hadn't really comprehended that the rest of the world still existed beyond the hospital walls, let alone that I could be sent home.

'But have those patients had caesareans too?'

'Oh, I've had caesareans!' By the time I formed the words to ask if her babies were born alive, she was gone, out of the room and off to manage the rest of the ward.

I started writing lists of the reasons why I couldn't be discharged just yet:
- because I can't get out of bed without assistance,
- because my partner is also injured and unable to care for me,
- because my able-bodied family members are already caring for my injured partner and two injured stepdaughters,
- because we don't have a home to go 'home' to.

I still looked pregnant and I was scared that well-meaning people would say things that would inadvertently break my heart. I planned a little preventative sign to wear:

*No, I'm not pregnant anymore.
My baby has died.*

•

I dreamt of a broken bathtub, of roadkill bathmats, of a chandelier constructed from tiny, dried-out bats, like muscatel grapes. I dreamt that I was at Rima's work, and was holding my yellow book with all my pregnancy medical records. Someone who didn't know about the accident saw my Transport Accident Commission form, printed with two little human outlines on it where the doctors could indicate my injuries, front and back. She mistook it for an ultrasound scan.

'Oh,' she said. 'You can see two of them in there—are you having twins?' I wasn't angry; I just cried, 'No, no, no, I've lost my baby.' Then someone offered to drive me home and I gave a scared moan: 'No, no, no; I don't want to go in a car.'

I dreamt that my hand was safe in my mum's hand, strong and warm. With fingers interlocked, we stretched our fingers out—hers more wrinkled but so similar in size and shape to mine. As I turned our facing hands, I saw her ring, middle and little fingers on one hand had been amputated above the first knuckle. They were smoothly healed, and strong, but incomplete. I cried out, 'Mama! What happened to your hand?' She gave me a sad look. 'Oh, that happened at work the other day.' I want to shake her. *Mama! No! No, this is not okay. Mama, you can't let this happen to you.* But she was right, it was too late to make a fuss. Nonetheless, I woke up crying. 'Mama—no, no!'

I had a jungle of flowers growing from the top of the cupboard in my room, a bit like Max's forest in *Where the Wild Things Are.*

•

Baby Lost

Sunday, 3 January 2010 nearly 1 a.m.

I was telling Matt the truth when I said I was not even thinking about the driver who caused the accident. He's an irrelevance to us now and to our recovery. What has happened has happened and getting angry at him will not change what we need to do to get better, and may make it harder.

I do remember that his name is Amrik—and so he must have a mother who brought him into the world, who held him and looked at his tiny face in wonder. And who gave him that name wishing only good things for him. I won't judge him (not that that is my job or in my power in any case) because I have driven stupidly too at times.

I know that on the Wednesday before we moved to Melbourne, I drove so fast and so angrily with the girls in the car that they were scared—just because I was angry and frustrated and impatient with Rima and with some difficulty with the move, I can't remember what. And Haloumi was in the car too, right there, below my angry heart, feeling all those stress chemicals circulate in my bloodstream. I thank God that the worst I did that day was upset my stepdaughters (that was bad enough) but I could have very easily caused an accident like the one which took our Khalila away. So, even if I can't control other people's driving, I promise never ever ever to drive when I'm that angry again.

I will stop the car, or not get into it, I will take a little walk or deep breaths, or smash plates, but I will not drive. I am scared to get in a car again—I will have to take that slowly.

•

My cousin Lou came to see me. We'd been to see her on the day of the accident. We'd kissed her goodbye at the gate, crossed the road to where our car was parked, pulled out from the kerb, turned left, then right, then left onto Warrigal Road, before being sucked into the black hole of the collision.

She hadn't told her kids yet that our baby died. They had come in while she was on the phone to her mum, my Aunty Helen. They heard her weep. 'Mummy, what's wrong?'

I pictured her in that lovely new kitchen, leaning on the bench where my pregnant belly touched the stone, where we ate Greek biscuits before getting in the car. She went down on her knees, gathered their little living bodies close, one in each arm, sniffed into their necks.

'There's been a car crash. You know Hannah and Rima and Jackie and Jasmin, who came over yesterday? Their car crashed and they were hurt.'

'Oh, Mummy!' said Connor. 'That baby must have been so scared.'

I hadn't wanted to think of this. I want to think that she felt loved all the way through, that she felt the bang, but knew I was still there with her, even if I couldn't protect her.

Tuesday, 5 January 2010 9 p.m.

Today was the day when everyone thought I was going crazy. No wonder really, when I tell them I'm writing a blockbuster novel which is going to be made into a movie starring Charlize Theron (as me, obviously) and Salma Hayek (as Rima) ('A heart-warming tale of tragedy, hope and incontinence' or 'Pollyanna on crack meets AB Facey'). Suddenly everyone was giving me worried looks—particularly when I insisted on writing down the names of every member of the hospital staff I met.

Here I was thinking that I had discovered a new post-accident Hannah with some inspiring new talents when everyone around me was thinking, 'She's dropped her bundle.' What shocked me was when the person from Epworth Rehabilitation came to assess me for a transfer to the rehabilitation hospital. I immediately wrote his name down in the yellow book—Kamal. He made jokes about being born in the seventies, but when we got down to it, told me that their primary concern for me was my neuro-psychological state.

We still had a holiday house on the Mornington Peninsula booked for the two weeks before our tenants were to move out. It was meant to be our babymoon—our reward for making it through the big move and Christmas, a little rest before we unpacked our house and got set up for the baby to arrive. When the doctors did their rounds, I asked whether we could still go. I wanted to feel the salt water wash over me. I wanted to hide a bit longer from Melbourne and any idea of 'normal' life.

'I don't think it's such a good idea,' the doctor said. 'This is the thing with internal bleeding—we take a three-three-three rule. For the first three days, there's a significant risk of further internal bleeding—that's why we kept you in ICU. For the next three weeks, the risk is reduced, but it's still quite serious. The risk reduces again after three weeks, but you've still got a higher-than-average risk of bleeding for the next three months.'

'How would I know if I was bleeding again? Would it hurt?'

'Not always. You can bleed to death without feeling much at all.'

A different nurse manager came to see me. His name was Ali. He admired the letter Jasmin had written to me, left-handed, as her right hand was still in a cast.

Dear Hannah
I'm so happy that your happy (ish) but just know that I'm here for you like how you were those past few years but yeah so is everyone else. I was so happy that I got to see you yesterday but yeah sorry I'm writing in my left hand!! My hand doesn't smell much anymore!! But it hurts. I love you see you chao from: Jasmin

He Blu-tacked it to the wall for me. 'I need to ask you a favour. We're looking at transferring you to rehab, but we've got a bit of an issue with rooms. Can I ask you to change to a shared room, just down the hall?'

I was grateful for any reprieve. My mum helped me pack up my things, piling bags and belongings on the bed, with me holding the vases of flowers. The photo the midwife gave me of Z was now in a glass frame Mum had bought from the hospital gift shop. I wrapped it carefully in her blankets, first one and then the other, and hugged it to my chest. The nurse released the brakes on the bed, and pushed us out of the room and down the hallway, like a little boat. Suddenly I felt the urge to document this. 'Mama, do you have your camera? Can we take some photos?'

The image of the bed piled with notebooks, colourful blankets and flowers, reminded me of Frida Kahlo, the surrealist artist I had been obsessed with as a teenager. When she was eighteen, Frida was on a bus on her way home to Coyoacán, Mexico City when it collided with a trolley car. She was thrown from the bus—and in the process was impaled on a handrail from the bus, which pierced her lower hip and came out her vagina. The impact fractured her pelvis, and broke her spine in three places, as well as her collarbone, two ribs and her right leg and foot. She was immobilised in a cast for a month, and underwent over thirty-five operations.[1] Frida's life, too, was pierced through with the after-effects of the accident—her health, her fertility (her injuries meant she was unable to carry a pregnancy to term) and her artwork.

Prior to the accident, she had ambitions to become a doctor, but 'bored as hell' in a hospital bed, she began painting. During her frequent convalescences she would often decorate her bed and the spinal casts or orthopaedic corsets she had to wear. Stuck in hospital or in bed, her portraits were primarily self-portraits—her gaze, level and direct, her brows, serious and meeting in the middle like a pair of raven's wings. Her portraiture was realist, down to the fine black hairs on her upper lip, but she interwove or surrounded her portraits with more surreal scenes. Frida's face appeared on the body of a deer, or suckling from a Pre-Columbian statute, or surrounded by flowers and monkeys. This was exactly what I wanted—to meet the horrors and indignities head-on, to examine them, and myself, and somehow to find beauty without smoothing out the painful parts or finding neat answers for unanswerable questions.

I had been at a loss as to how to understand myself as injured and grieving while still maintaining some measure of dignity. So I took Frida as my patron saint, as my survival mentor, as inspiration to look my circumstances directly in the eye and to document my pain with an artist's curiosity. My life in Frida-vision suddenly seemed artistically surreal rather than dangerously crazy.

In the new room, I felt the need to keep the rails on the bed up, as though this bed-boat that had carried me here might at any moment lurch and roll, bellied by a big dark ocean. I drew a ship in my notebook, with Z as the anchor, and wrote the words of another Little Birdy song on the sail.

> Who's going to love you now, baby?
> Who's going to love you now, baby?
> When you're done fighting that war at sea
> Get on that ship and sail back to me!

Penny came to visit again. She climbed up onto the bed with me, and I showed her the ship drawing and together we wept.

I called my mum and wept again. 'Mama, I just need to stop for a minute. I need to stop and wipe the phone because I'm crying so much that I'm scared I'll electrocute myself.' This, for me, counted as a good laugh—that and announcements over the PA system about returning the bladder scanner to level five—and for a little while, I shook with both tears and laughter. 'Mama, I'm not a person at all, I'm just a force of nature,' I said. I pictured the *Pasha Bulker*, the container ship washed up on Nobbys Beach in Newcastle in the big storm of June 2007. On our way north for a hockey carnival, we had stayed the night in an onsite van at a Newcastle motel, feeling the storm shake the thin walls. We woke and drove into town, passing cars made flotsam by the floods, with high-tide marks of dirt and leaves reaching their windows. And there on the beach, tall as an eight-storey building, was the *Pasha Bulker*, the surf lapping it, but dwarfing the beach pavilions, and commanding an audience of surprised-looking adults and kids still in pyjamas.

My hysterical laughter slowed to sobs. 'Mama, I don't know how I'm going to sleep.'

On the other end of the phone, my mum spoke softly. 'When I was in the Alfred and had trouble sleeping, the women there gave me something to say which I could repeat to make myself feel safe and calm.'

She meant the psych unit at the Alfred Hospital, where she had spent uncounted weeks in late 1987 after a particularly bad bout of depression. This was not a usual topic of conversation for her.

My brother and I had been in primary school, and while Mum was in hospital, our art teacher, Miss Komis, would drive us home from school. 'Call me Fifi,' she said, and sometimes took us out for ice-creams on the way home, as a treat. I would sit in the front passenger seat of her cobalt-blue car, touching my finger to each unfamiliar object: the perforated leather of the door handle, the chrome door latch, the glove box. The more practical details of that time are fuzzy. How long was Mum in hospital for? Who looked after our little sister, who was not at school yet? But I clearly remember the piles of cicada shells my brother and I collected each afternoon after Fifi dropped us home, and the vinyl chairs in the hospital's TV room when we visited. Everything was hushed there, and Mum was even quieter than she'd been in the weeks leading up to her hospitalisation. She looked half-transparent, as though she had lost the will to be seen. At home, I was a bossy, responsible big sister. I helped Dad cook dinner and do the shopping, and I referred to my brother and sister, five and seven years younger than me, as 'the littlies'.

'The phrase they gave me,' Mum continued, 'was, "I wrap this pure white cloak around me through which nothing can harm me and only goodness may pass".'

I repeated it back to Mum several times. I liked the idea of a cloak filtering out harm, permeable only to goodness. But I wasn't convinced that anything could protect me, or those I loved, anymore.

I was conscious that, now that I was sharing, I shouldn't keep my poor roommate awake, but I couldn't figure out how to stop the weeping and laughing and writing. I asked the nurses again whether I could see a counsellor. Several hours later, a volunteer arrived. Just as well—on one of my many lists for the day, I'd written, 'If no psych assessment by 5pm, DRAW ON MONOBROW.'

Pat was older, quietly spoken and wore a smart suit with a brooch. She wasn't sure whether she could help, but encouraged me onto my crutches and out into the hallway, further than I'd been in my whole time there. Pushing back the boundaries of the known universe, we found a corner with two chairs, and she patted my arm. We formulated a plan that didn't involve weeping all night and she walked me back to the ward. I pulled up the sides on the bed, invoked Frida, covered myself with hand-knitted baby blankets, pushed the ivory bangle up my arm and set sail for the night.

7
Tabloid tragedy

My sister let slip that there was a story about us in the paper. I could always trust her not to filter information for me.

I asked for a copy and Rima obliged, buying one from the hospital newsagency and bringing it up to the ward. I wasn't prepared for it to be the front-page headline. Our story wasn't just our story anymore; suddenly, it was a 'tragedy', for people to tut over on their tea break. Part of me felt vindicated. I wanted our loss to be important—everyone should know we had lost our baby daughter. How could anything hurt this much and not be front-page news?

But it also felt very odd to have everything that had happened to us in the past days reduced to twelve characters of thick black headline. They had also got it wrong. 'LOST IVF ANGEL'. She wasn't IVF conceived. And Rima was not, as was reported, my sister-in-law. I felt ill at ease. I was conscious that the pedestal for tragic, wronged mothers is a narrow and unsteady one, surrounded by a sea of condemnation for 'bad' mothers. I knew from growing up with seeing Lindy Chamberlain on the television that it all could turn very quickly. I didn't have an unusual religion; I had the benefit of white, middle-class privilege; and now the *Herald Sun* had incorrectly extended me the benefits of presumed heterosexuality. Did I really want to poke that bear?

When I had a gap between visitors at lunchtime, I called the *Herald Sun* news desk and asked to speak to the journalist: 'The front-page story from today is about me, and it contains factual errors. I want a correction published.' They put me through to the journalist, and when I told him off for his inaccuracies, he was contrite, and wanted to make it right.

'I'll do better than a correction,' he said. 'I can do another story.'

Suddenly he seemed a little too eager to put it right—and he was offering to come in and talk to me. 'I need to think about this,' I said. I gave him Mum's phone number, deliberately creating a buffer zone.

When I told family members I'd been in touch with a journalist, there was some alarm, particularly given my recent crazy-lady antics. Apparently, a journalist had turned up at my dad's house, pressing him for comment, and my dad and stepmum had had to keep the phone off the hook. Over the next few days, I consulted with my friend Matt, a journo, about what to do.

In the meantime, I had to pack. I was being transferred to a rehabilitation hospital. I was triumphant about not being sent home yet. Mum helped me shower. It was complicated. I covered my left leg, splint and all, in a garbage bag, propped it on one chair and sat on another. Mum left to let me dry myself and start getting dressed. I took my time. There was a lot to look at, seeing my body naked.

Black and dark purple bruises blossomed, like tropical botanical illustrations, from my elbows to my fingertips, cascaded down my thighs, and nestled, deepest of all, in a seatbelt stripe across my chest. The dark, dead blood collected in strange patterns—sheet marks, the creases of my wrist, the waffle pattern of a wound dressing, in the lines of the old scar from my kidney operation. This was a kind of bodily print-making practice. My left breast hung heavy, covered in one big bruise that faded to yellow at my cleavage.

When Rima came in, I had a new favour to ask her. 'Can you take photos of all the bruises? They'll disappear soon—I need to remember this.' She was systematic about it, starting with my feet and working her way up. 'There's one behind your right ear; maybe from your glasses?' I posed, pointing to the bruises, like the saints in Renaissance paintings touching their wounds. *Look. Here. Proof.* What did it mean, to photograph this naked, bruised body? Was it pornography? Crime-scene photography? Art? I didn't know what to do with my face in these photos. Sometimes I smiled. Sometimes I looked away.

To catch the full colours of the bruising, I had to hold my arms out in front of me, hands up. When Rima showed me the photos, I saw a woman trying to defend herself.

When the nurses came to change the dressings, I got the camera out. I wanted to see what was under all those patches. This body, which had been mine for thirty-three years, was unfamiliar to me. On my right ankle, two staples held shut a small but deep incision, alongside a U-shaped cut. In the fleshy bit of my forearm, a small wound was still weeping where they had pulled out a long shard of glass. Several big dressings covered my left knee, and I could feel the staples underneath making three quarters of a circle around the knee cap. The surgeon had joked that I'd have a hammer and sickle scar. My communist left leg. Ha ha. Rima took fuzzy photos of the lumpy scar on my head—pink, and still stitched with thick black thread.

As systematic as Rima's photos were, they were not enough. I borrowed my mum's camera, and shut myself in the bathroom. My supply of Rima's t-shirts had run out, so I had been wearing two hospital gowns, one on forwards and one on backwards, to avoid the unflattering gap. It was the sartorial equivalent of a kidney dish—without my own clothes, jewellery or make-up, and in the starkness of the hospital bathroom, my body looked like a medical specimen.

The morning of my transfer, I picked out a kaftan-like green and white dress from the bag of Mum's clothes she had brought in for me so I didn't need to wear my maternity clothes. I tied the hot pink belt from my dressing gown above my still-big post-partum belly. I tied my hair back and put on make-up. I held Mum's ivory bangle to my lips, inhaling its smell and invoking the elephant whose life was claimed in making it. *Elephant—I'm so sorry. Please haunt me, please protect my baby girl, wherever she is.* I sticky-taped a sign to my belly: 'I'm not pregnant anymore. My baby has died.' I knew it was unlikely that anyone would comment, but the thought that people might see me and think I was still pregnant was unbearable. I needed to open a window on this stifling pain, let others peer in.

•

The week before we'd come down to Melbourne for Christmas, Mum had stayed with us in Sydney and we'd gone shopping in Newtown. In a small shop full of beautiful things, she had bought an oval enamel brooch with a matryoshka face on it, like a little doll. At the time, I'd felt covetous. It was a beautiful, expensive object, exactly the kind of thing I couldn't justify buying when we were relocating interstate and about to have a baby. But the matryoshka brooch reappeared while I was in the trauma unit, Mum slipping it wordlessly into my hand. The enamel was solid yet silky-soft, and the small baby face, with a blue asterisk on each cheek, smiled at me. In the shop, it had just looked cute and smiley. Now I assumed the asterisks were tears. I pushed the pin through my clothes, and then through my bra, so I could feel the cool metal of the clasp against my breast, always on the left side, over my heart. *Here you are, my little one.*

•

When the orderlies arrived to transfer me by ambulance, I was chipper. 'We're working on the theory that you're taking me to rehab in a hovercraft,' I said. 'So it can just float up and out of the way of any accident. Does that sound okay?' They were reassuring. They thought I was having a joke with them.

Mum came with me. I held her hand as the trolley clicked into place and the doors were closed. I blinked slowly as we emerged into daylight and the world beyond my hospital bubble. Through the venetian blinds of the ambulance, I could see streets, trees, traffic, all behaving as though nothing had happened. This time we travelled without the sirens. This time, the outcome was known. There was no great rush.

•

In my room in the rehab hospital, I met the nurses and told my story. Then the doctor, then the physio; lunch; then the psychologist, the occupational therapist, and the other doctor. By 5 p.m., I had told our accident six times over, and by the time Rima arrived, my compliance was gone. Everything felt wrong, and suddenly I was white-hot with anger—at this stupid hospital, at the other driver, at myself for thinking this was all somehow fixable if only I behaved correctly, at Mum and Rima for being there and not being able to fix any of it. I was contrary, inconsolable. The air-conditioning was on too high, the mattress was too soft and I missed the nurses from Royal Melbourne. Mum and Rima didn't know what to do. Take photos, I told them, and then I gave them the finger when they did. I was sorry, though, when visiting hours were over, and they had to go, so that it was just me and the photos of Z in my new room. I stayed up late drawing a diagram of myself, with arrows explaining my injuries and my family relationships, to be stuck onto the door of my room so that I wouldn't need to explain it all to anyone else.

At 7 a.m. my phone buzzed with a text message. It was from my friend Kana, announcing the safe arrival of her baby girl. I wept, and plucked tissue after tissue from the box on the nightstand, with the 'robot arm' the occupational therapist had given me, just to hear the tearing sound they made as they came out of the box. The information echoed around my heart like a loose spanner in an empty toolbox. I logged onto Facebook for the pictures. Here were the photos of Kana and me at her baby shower only a few weeks ago, standing belly to belly. And here was her baby daughter, alive and safe in her arms; my baby, dust. I wrote my own Facebook post.

Baby Lost

7 January 2010

What happened is still so raw and new that we are wrapping our heads around a new bit of it every day. And also failing to wrap our heads around, and howling at that failure and our loss and the fact that our daughter will never open her beautiful eyes to see the people who love her more than anything. An inaccurate version of what happened was on the front cover of a tabloid newspaper. This is my response to it:

> Letter to the Editor
> Eleven days ago I was 34 weeks pregnant and driving home with my defacto wife in the passenger seat and my beloved stepdaughters in the back seat. A four-wheel drive came onto our side of the road and hit us. We were all badly hurt but our baby daughter died in my womb from the impact. My defacto wife (I can't call her my wife because in this country we cannot marry) and I had spent nearly four years getting to know our sperm donor, undertaking tests and trying to get me pregnant using assisted conception (fortunately we did not need IVF). When the *Herald Sun* reported the accident and our loss on 28 December 2009, ('LOST IVF ANGEL'), it mistakenly called her my 'sister-in-law' and referred to my stepdaughters vaguely as 'two children'. Many people reading your article must have been wondering about the relationships between a pregnant woman, her sister-in-law and these two children who were all hurt in the one car. I just need to clarify—we are a family. My defacto wife (what a clunky phrase that is) and I lost our little girl, and our big girls lost their baby sister. I don't want our family to be invisible—we have enough pain and injuries to deal with at the moment.

But in this strange movie which is apparently now my life, the most genuine and real thing is the love we have felt around us from family, friends, and also people who may not know us in real life but have very real compassion for us (or worse, have been through equally heartbreaking things themselves). It is huge, and we feel so warmed by your love but at the moment we are still so broken—physically, and in our hearts, that we can't respond to all the messages. I am out of ICU (yay), out of the trauma ward (yay), and in rehab. I hate being here—but am doing my best to heal and learn how to do basic things so I can get home and be with my beautiful girls and do the rest of my healing there. Rima & girls are out of hospital (yay), but there are still various stages to go.

We will never ever be the same after this. I could never have imagined that the Haloumi who kicked and hiccuped inside me could be such a beautiful little baby girl. If the impact had not abrupted the placenta she would have been fine and things would be so different. I am so proud of her and so so heart-broken. Thank you for your thoughts and love.

We will be having a 40 days memorial at some stage—possibly early Feb when she was due. Forty days is significant within Rima's faith. For forty days the soul wrestles with itself and its good and bad deeds in the desert, before moving on (though we're pretty sure our girl didn't have a bad deed to her name). If you are able to join us, we would love it so much. I warn you it is going to be very sad. We will have a weeping competition and I will win. The pay-off is you will get to see pictures of the most beautiful grumpy baby girl in the world.

•

One morning in rehab, I had a phone call from the police officer handling our case. He'd spoken to a number of witnesses and it was clear that it hadn't been the Pajero driver's fault at all. The collision had started, he said, with an older-model Commodore, whose driver was involved in some kind of road-rage altercation with another car. Several kilometres back, the Commodore driver, a uni student, had slowed down and stopped in a no-stopping zone to drop off a friend. The driver behind objected, hooted his horn, overtook the Commodore in an aggressive way, and was seen shaking his fist and yelling at the Commodore driver. In response, the Commodore driver sped up and tried to overtake aggressively in turn, but he didn't get the chance to yell anything, because he didn't check his blindspot when overtaking and failed to see the Pajero in the next lane. The flanks of the two cars made contact, knocking the Pajero onto our side of the road.

It took me a few moments to process this news. The Pajero driver was not at fault. His car was just a big, heavy billiard ball tapped in our direction.

In the aftermath of the collision, witnesses saw the Commodore slow down and pull over briefly, but while other drivers around us were stopping to render assistance, the Commodore driver drove off, and returned the car to his brother's house. When the police traced the car's number plate to that address and arrested him, he told them he had fled the scene of the accident because he was fearful of the other driver involved in the road-rage incident. He was charged with five counts of dangerous driving causing serious injury (one each for me, Rima, Jasmin, Jackie and for the driver of the Pajero) and one count of failing to stop at the scene of an accident, and was released on bail. Because she was stillborn, there was no charge for dangerous driving causing Z's death. 'Serious injury' didn't come close to describing our loss, but I was okay with her coming under my jurisdiction rather than that of the *Crimes Act*.

I sent my letter to the journalist, and, as promised, he spun it into another front-page story. I sticky-taped the front page to my door in rehab, with a drawn-in apostrophe correcting it from 'Mum's Pain' to 'Mums' Pain'. The article also reported on the bail application, at which the police prosecutor argued there was a risk the defendant would try to leave the country while on bail, citing the example of another Indian student, Puneet Puneet, who fled in June 2009 after pleading guilty to culpable driving causing death and negligently causing serious injury.

Bail was granted but, nonetheless, our case fed into the mounting tension between the Victoria Police and the Indian community in Melbourne, over perceptions that police were failing to respond adequately to a spike in violence and race hate incidents against Indian people. A string of murders and assaults on Indians in Melbourne through 2008 and 2009 had prompted the Indian government to issue a travel warning for citizens considering studying in Australia, and sparked protests in Melbourne and New Delhi. In this climate, many journalists described the driver who caused our accident not as 'a student' but as 'an Indian national'. I had a queasy feeling as I realised that our story played neatly into racist stereotypes of a white woman (and, worse still, a pregnant one) harmed by a brown man.

•

Each day in rehab, I was booked to work with the physio for an hour or two. I would go on my crutches down the corridor and to the 'gym', which was less like a gym and more like a surrealist kindergarten. There was play equipment for adults, parallel ballet barres, a play kitchen, and a rail with clothes hanging on it (dress-ups?), along with fit balls and yoga mats. And then there was the thing I averted my eyes from. I knew it was there because I had seen it the first time I walked into the gym and felt a jolt of fear through my gut. A weepy, elongated sigh escaped from me. I knew that, at some point, the physio would move me towards it. It was a dismembered car—just the front half, so that you could practise getting in and out of it on either the driver or passenger sides. As the physio taught me how to tackle stairs on crutches, I arranged my ascent and descent so that I didn't have to look in that direction. The steps led up to a clothes line, and with each ascent I triumphantly moved a peg from one line to the other, with an absurdist flourish.

To add to the surrealist effect, one day I arrived in the gym to find my Year Twelve English teacher there, also being coached by a physio. We were like racehorses, being nudged along by our minders. We couldn't chat properly but I got enough of my story out for her to get it.

'I hope you're writing, Hannah.'

I assured her I was, and she made me memorise her email address so that I could write to her.

8
Permission to bend

The accident, and the long hours that followed of ambulance, emergency room, labour and then waking from surgery to see our daughter, had obliterated the normal markers of daytime, nighttime or mealtimes. Time started again from zero—everything was measured in hours, and then days, since the accident. In rehab, I started reconnecting myself with 'outside' time, looking at the newspaper each day and marvelling that people's lives went on regardless of our catastrophe.

One of the elephants at Melbourne Zoo was due to give birth to a calf any day now, and I followed the story, terrified that her baby too might die. The article recounted a statistic that made my heart ache for elephant mothers. For elephants giving birth in captivity, there was an extraordinarily high stillbirth rate, particularly for first babies. I thought of mother elephant eyes, weary with sorrow, and of a mother elephant trunk, searching out and touching on the still, hairy form of her baby, and wept my own elephant tears.

While I was eating my breakfast one morning, I drew rows of wonky boxes in my diary so that I could count the days. It was a double calendar. Each box had two numbers: the date and how many days since our own ground zero. Just writing the number '27'—the date of the accident—made me shudder and cry. I dripped strawberry jam on that box and drew a sad face beneath. It didn't quite capture the violence of that day, but I couldn't leave it unmarked. I'd had plans for these dates. These were to be days in a rented holiday house, lazy walks to and from the beach, with time to decide on a name for this baby, and to recover from the interstate move before we moved into our house and set up a nursery. By numbering those boxes, by stitching together these beautiful summer dates with our new messed-up reality, I inserted myself back into time, and was no longer in the suspended, timeless world of hospital.

I'd been discharged from Royal Melbourne with various letters (so much paperwork, getting hit by a car!), including one confirming that I had an appointment with the orthopaedic surgeon who had operated on my knee. That and my hoped-for discharge date were the only goalposts I could work towards at that moment.

I was so sick of rehab that the thought of an excursion, even if it involved more doctors, was vaguely appealing. Mum came with me, holding my hand in the back of the ambulance. Cars and traffic still terrified me, but the hovercraft delusion was holding up reasonably well. The ambulance driver was friendly, and I felt more like a well-treated parcel than an injured person by the time he delivered Mum and me to the patient transport lounge at Royal Melbourne. Appointment letter in hand, we followed coloured lines painted on the lino floor to find the right lift, the right floor, and eventually the right waiting room.

I sat in it with Mum and a variety of recently operated-on people, while the doctors and hospital staff moved around us. 'I am a patient,' I thought. 'This is what we do: we wait patiently, we move slowly.' I had a moment of horror when I recognised one of the surgeons. He'd been in the same year as me at college but studying medicine. I'd felt a tiny bit of pride on getting to Royal Melbourne without a major freak-out, despite the horror I still felt at cars, but suddenly I imagined how he might have seen me—as another patient on crutches, dressed in loud colours, or maybe just as a fairly standard knee injury. Thankfully, it wasn't he who called out my name, but another young surgeon, with a dapper suit and piles of curly hair.

Before he would see me, the surgeon sent in a nurse to undo the staples that had held my skin together. She spent some time hunting around in drawers and cupboards until she emerged triumphant with what looked like a giant pair of plastic preschool scissors with the tips bent in sinister-looking ways. She angled a spotlight at my knee and, one by one, removed the staples, leaving little red dots either side of the thick pink scar that curved around my kneecap. I asked Mum to take photos. They came out more theatrically than I expected, a rubber-gloved hand hanging in the spotlight above my newly unstapled knee.

The nurse piled the staples in a yellow plastic kidney dish. I eyed them off and had visions of taking them to a jeweller, and asking them to make a short chain from all these wonky 'W's—maybe enough for a bracelet? They'd held me together for nearly three weeks. I wasn't sure I was ready to let them go.

'Is it okay if I keep the staples?' I asked the nurse.

She wrinkled her nose slightly and smiled. For her, they were medical waste.

'I don't think so, but I can ask for you.'

She bustled out, and Mum and I sat there, waiting for the doctor.

I engaged in a short thought experiment, based on a popular reality TV show that I used to call 'my life'. It involved not catastrophic injuries, grief and prodding by medical professionals but standing up in front of my contracts law class, talking to them about implied duties of good faith. How to bring colour and movement to the crucial High Court case of *Hospital Products v United States Surgical Corporation*? Why not show them some photos of my knee, with thirty-three surgical staples, just like the kind the defendant had promised to distribute on behalf of the US manufacturer but decided to repackage as his own product? There was something macabre about this thought, about plucking a teachable moment from the wreckage that the accident had wrought on our lives. At the same time, I felt ruthless. The accident took so much from us, why couldn't I take a little back?

Suddenly, the surgeon was there, in his slim-tailored suit, the fabric creasing expensively around his own highly operational knees as he sat down on the swivel chair and riffled through my file. My leg was laid out on the bench, the velcro straps of the brace undone around it, but I had to swing it down so I could turn and face him.

'There wasn't a scan from before the surgery, was there?' he asked, without introducing himself.

'No, no … I don't think so.'

'Okay then; well, let's have a look.'

He briefly examined my knee, made a quick note and pronounced he shouldn't need to see me again.

'And you shouldn't need that brace anymore,' he added.

'But, um, will I be able to bend it again?' I queried.

'Yes, yes, of course—the physio will help you with that.'

And that was it.

As I gathered my crutches and bags and returned to the waiting room, I felt a little like Dorothy at the end of *The Wizard of Oz*. 'You mean all I needed to do all along was click my heels together and say, "There's no place like home"?'

It was somewhere in another queue—after we'd taken a wrong turn down another winding corridor—that I wept. The lino changed colour here. Corridors of one building joined to an older building, with old-fashioned skirting boards. It was as though the new hospital had swallowed the old one whole.

I'd circled this day on the calendar. It had pulled me forward as some kind of marker, some way to differentiate one babyless week from another. I'd started the day chipper. This was a step on my way out of rehab, on my way home. I'd dressed smartly, felt like I was carrying off the pretence of being a normal, capable adult. Once these staples were out, I had reasoned, I would be able to have a bath or go for a swim. In rehab I had been able to put myself together each morning—piece new outfits together from my new 'Crippled but Quirky' collection and propel myself out into the thin simulacrum of the world that was rehab's public spaces. And today we had braved vehicular transport, and navigated the long corridors of the Royal Melbourne Hospital to find the very dapper orthopaedic surgeon who granted me permission to bend.

I'd wanted the staples out, but the thought of bending, of walking unaided, of returning to this noisy, busy world that was so sharp with reminders of our loss, felt exhausting. My carefully gathered energy had brought me this far, but the lino corridors defeated me. I crumpled and wept. Mum held my hand, gathered me in a little, and then we went and found a wheelchair. We asked for directions, found another waiting room, and made it through the last appointment with the trauma consultant on the promise of a cuppa. I was relieved when Mum navigated us back to the caf. She went to buy the tea, and I looked around and realised that just over there was where we'd sat and drunk coffee after Z's funeral; and there, just down that corridor, not 20 metres away, was the room where I'd pulled that small, solid box onto my lap and kissed her cold face.

Part II
RE-ENTRY

9
Zombieland

Coming 'home' to our new house on Bayliss Street in the flat expanses of Melbourne's northern suburbs, nothing was familiar. In a matter of weeks, we had lost our home, our city, our jobs, our baby daughter and all our plans and hopes for her. We'd also lost our car, each of us had experienced significant physical injury, and our surviving children had lost their school and contact with their friends and extended family. No wonder I felt like an alien, as I crutched my way around our new neighbourhood. And if I, who was originally a Melbourne person and had all my family and old friends here, felt like an alien, how much more alien did Rima and the girls feel?

While I was in rehab, they had been staying at my dad and stepmum's place. Mum was living in her mobile home, which was parked in their driveway, and my brother Jeremy was sleeping in the rumpus room. It was like some extreme blended-family in-law reality TV challenge. Not only did they have to live with one another, grieve and recover, but my parents also needed to ferry Rima and the girls around to numerous medical appointments, visit me in rehab, and help us get ready to move into the Bayliss Street house.

Rima's day surgery to insert a metal plate into her hand was helpfully scheduled for the same day as surgery for Jackie's broken nose. Dad and my stepmum, Deb, arranged for my brother to drop Rima off at hospital on his way to a job, while they stayed with Jackie. Concerned that Rima would wake up from the anaesthetic alone and with no transport, I rang my friend Bins, who answered the phone at 7 a.m. and rushed out of bed to be there, Diet Coke in hand, when Rima woke up. As soon as Rima was released from post-op recovery, Bins ferried her over to my rehab hospital, both of them in good spirits. Rima, still dozy from the anaesthetic, fell asleep on my bed, and, mistaking her for me, the nurses tried to give her my painkillers.

In rehab, I was taking more and more photos; fewer of my bruises, and more of my face. I couldn't quite recognise this face. Something had changed. I pored over my face in the photos of me holding Zainab the morning she was born. The puffiness and blood-red hair were now gone, but when I looked in the mirror, my eyes had not returned to normal. There was a weariness, a knowledge, there that I didn't have before. I felt haunted—my body had been the scene of a death. I had carried death within me and birthed her. I needed to catch what traces remained on my face of the moment when her small soul flickered out from within my living one. How did her soul escape my body? Where did she go, and how much of my own soul did she take with her? Scrolling through the photos on Rima's camera, I saw something. Two shots where I had accidentally held the button down and closed my eyes. I flicked back and forth. Eyes open, eyes closed. Eyes open, eyes closed. Like an old-fashioned doll that you tilt to make her blink, lifelike but lifeless, blinking in disbelief. The image jumped slightly. This was not real life, just a photographic trick.

I'd never found horror movies to be up my alley but I now felt an empathy for the zombies, dazed and numbed by death. They don't know what has happened, and are still trying to work it out. Something terrible befell them, but they're still here, moving and apparently alive. Every now and then, I would wonder if I hadn't also died in the accident; that this was some dream or neural flicker.

After my clothes had been cut from me in emergency, and I'd spent my ICU days in half-undone hospital gowns, being able to wear proper clothes was re-humanising. The act of choosing my outfits became a ritual. I couldn't wear the same things I'd worn before—my post-partum body still couldn't fit into my non-maternity clothes—but I couldn't bring myself to wear the same maternity outfits that I'd worn only a few weeks ago. Instead, I tied scarves or soft fabric belts around my hair, like Alice bands; I put bright colours together, Frida-style. My mum lent me clothes from her eclectic wardrobe. I sought out big jewellery. I wore big red plastic earrings made from recycled monkeys in a barrel, my aqua scarf around my head, a soft grey shirt dress tied with the hot pink belt from my bathrobe. With make-up, I reclaimed my face from grief and the hospital environment.

Mum sallied forth with my absurdist shopping lists:

- doorstop
- bra
- underwear (high waisted)
- sticky tape or glue
- *Where the Wild Things Are*
- coloured textas or pencils
- more fruit
- Charlize Theron

I needed high-waisted underpants that wouldn't irritate my caesar scar; bras that were soft-cupped, but not maternity bras. Nanna underwear, it turns out, is the gentlest. Mum found bras for me that were designed for women undergoing breast cancer treatment. As I dressed, I felt solidarity for those women, sent them my love.

If I was demanding of family members, I was positively bolshie with the nursing staff. In retuning to this baby-like state, I had realised that it matters a lot how gently (or otherwise) caregivers provided their care. When you are dependent on others, small things can upset your routines, and familiar ways of doing things are inordinately comforting.

I'd gone from a public teaching hospital with high nurse–patient ratios to a private suburban rehab centre with low ratios. Many other patients here were elderly and for them this was probably a step on the way into a nursing home. The night nurse often told me off for staying up late, and one night, without asking, she turned the lights out when I was awake and writing. I was outraged, and asked my mum to bring in a small lamp so that I had my own light source.

I'd been given a mattress with an extra-soft section at the foot, designed to avoid heel pressure sores for elderly people with paper-thin skin. But it meant that the weight of my foot pulled at my broken knee. When an ordinary mattress wasn't forthcoming after a few days, I picked up my bedding and napped on the floor; much more comfortable. I awoke to the nurse manager freaking out. Incident reports had to be filed, I got a stern talking to, and a new mattress arrived that afternoon.

The police officer handling our case had visited me in hospital once. He was an older bloke—small but wiry, and with an unironic moustache. 'Were you wearing a seatbelt?' he'd asked in an accusing tone.

My hand shot up to my chest, and the bruises that the seatbelt had left. 'Yes; yes, I was.'

When he returned to see me again in rehab, I was in bed. I asked when we might be able to do my police statement. I wanted it done before I was discharged, so we could start a new chapter in our new home with, at least, our part in the criminal investigation resolved. His preference was to do it once I was at home, so that we'd be uninterrupted. He was testy. 'I've already got people on my case, complaining about keeping him in custody over a week because he's an Indian student.'

His remark got my lawyer hackles up—the driver who caused our accident had to answer for his actions, not for his cultural heritage. But I wasn't going to engage in that debate with the police officer in front of me; we just needed to sort out how this interview was going to happen. I asked what information he'd need, so I could make notes, and he spat back, 'You should know, you're a lawyer.' We went back and forth, and suddenly he was yelling, telling me that we'd do this interview on *his* terms, not mine. I agreed—anything to get him out of my space. I was shaken, and hot with shame.

The friends who were renting our new house had arranged to vacate it a few days early. Our furniture was already there, waiting for us in the shed, but neither Rima nor I were physically able to move it. So I put the call out on Facebook, and suddenly we had a schedule of helpers, assembling furniture, moving beds, stocking our fridge. Moving day coincided with my second-last day in rehab, so that I would have a properly assembled bed to come home to the next day.

While friends shifted our furniture, Jeremy sat with me in an interview room at the rehab hospital for my police interview, this time with the head of the collisions unit. After the incident with the leading officer on our case, I'd called and requested that someone else interview me. Jeremy sat with me and listened, giving a silent hand squeeze when I needed it.

On my last night in rehab, I stayed up late writing, despite the night nurse making firm and sensible suggestions about getting some sleep. The light from the small lamp Mum had brought in for me bounced off the mirrored frame around Z's picture, sending small spirals and leaves across the wall.

Thursday, 14 January 2010

Oh, my little one. I wanted to be setting up our house to be babysafe, not Zimmer-frame safe. I wanted your cot in our lovely front bedroom, where the bay window lets the light in, not physiotherapy equipment to help me lift my poor leg and reach for things. I was sick of rehab, and delighted at the thought of being in our own space, but I was also terrified of leaving my bubble and re-entering 'real life' without a Haloumi in my belly or a baby in my arms.

The next morning, my dad and stepmum came to take me home. I sat in the back of the car, my sore leg lying across the bench seat. The traffic made me nervous. All these death-machines, pacing in our midst like semi-tamed tigers, and everyone but me oblivious to their teeth and claws. I held on, and we made tense little jokes about hovercrafts. When we arrived, Dad helped me out of the car, giving me my crutches so I could meet Rima on the threshold, with tears and an embrace.

I sat on a chair in the garden—our garden—in the northern sun, and our little dog, Eddie, leapt up onto my lap. Big dog Atari would have leapt up too, were it not for Rima protecting me from his enthusiasm. The dogs and cat had spent a much longer holiday than expected at the kennels where we'd dropped them off just before Christmas. In the sterile, shiny hospital space, I had missed their abundant furriness, and their wordless, boundless affection.

That first day at home was razor sharp. It was so perfect in every way except one. Here was the room we'd dreamt of, but where was the cot? Here was the garden I'd always wanted, but no small feet to take their first steps on the grass. It felt like a grisly nursery rhyme from an era when death was mundane enough to feature in children's games: 'down will fall baby, cradle and all.' When friends came to help with the unpacking, weariness hit me and I slunk back into bed to hide and weep. I'd always been relentlessly sociable, but now I prioritised my own need for quiet. I couldn't explain this and I couldn't make it nice.

When I started unpacking, I found the jumper I'd worn on the day of the accident. Unlike all the other clothes I'd worn that day, it hadn't become bloodstained or been cut up, because I'd taken it off before we got in the car. I held it up to my body and looked in the mirror. The jumper was slack and flabby from where my big, taut belly had been. *This*, I told my weeping self, *this is proper crazy-lady grief.* A small, mean voice in my head wanted to call it histrionics, to slap myself out of it, but this grief was bigger and more elemental than anything I could put into words.

That night was the first since the accident that Rima and I could sleep in one bed together. Unlike the surreal one in ICU when she'd slept on two chairs pushed together beside my bed, we could embrace properly. We held onto one another, shipwreck survivors in a salty ocean of tears.

10

The 'born alive' rule

Home didn't quite feel like home those first few weeks—here were our familiar things but oriented differently in a new, unfamiliar space. Our bed in Sydney had faced the door, but here friends had assembled our bed next to the door. My entire life had been turned 90 degrees; everything was off-kilter. I had to remember the way to the bathroom. I noted down each medication I took. It felt remiss suddenly to live unmonitored after all the heart rate monitors and oxygen saturation clips that we'd relied on for proof that I was alive.

Saturday, 23 January 2010

It's 4 a.m. and I'm awake again—thinking of her being cut from my body. Four weeks ago today was Boxing Day. A day to sleep in—or in my case, wake up, eat enormous pregnant woman breakfast, then go back to bed.

At that point, we hadn't even decided whether or not to go to that stupid picnic on the 27th—our fate was still open. I know I'm torturing myself, but I still wish we'd decided not to go. All I wanted from that day was to hang out with my mum for a bit, do as little as possible and enjoy being pregnant after all the crazy moving interstate and Christmas business. Why did I feel the need to drive around seeing people?

Four a.m. would still find me awake most nights. I'd started reading again, frightening myself with the dystopian future Margaret Atwood created in *The Year of the Flood* and making things worse. Some nights I'd call friends living overseas to quell the rising tide of my own fear and panic. There I was, limping around the bathroom floor in my summer nightie at four in the morning, ranting like a madwoman to my dear friend Will while he was at work in a London law firm.

Our days were structured around appointments: physio, psychologist, occupational therapist. In between, we unpacked and worked towards two dates: the girls' first day at their new school, and Z's memorial on 7 February, to mark *al Arba'een*—forty days since her death and the end of the initial period of intense mourning. As it turned out, it also corresponded with her due date; the week I had imagined I'd be waddling around, impatient for her to be born.

I was avoiding the *why* question whenever it popped into my head. The newspapers Dad had brought me in hospital were full of pictures of the Haiti earthquake—more senseless trauma and loss. I could remember that feeling of being crushed. Among the people buried in rubble, was there a pregnant woman? For me, it had only been a matter of minutes of being crushed and trapped before I knew that fire and ambulance crews were on their way to free me. Meanwhile, earthquake victims were trapped, half-crushed, for days, and with no certainty of good medical care if they were freed. Their pain and loss, unlike mine, were compounded by poverty, and indifference from those who could afford to help.

At home, I started creating more of the blinking portraits, using Photoshop to create animated portraits punctuated with sighs, swallows and blinks. The image would jump unnaturally, disclosing that it was a trick, a sleight-of-hand substitute for the real thing. These moving

The 'born alive' rule

portraits were my own little robots, helping me carry out the weary waiting and time-marking of grief. I created loops of thirty-three, thirty-four, twenty-seven or twelve seconds, putting to work the numbers that still buzzed in my head—my age, Z's gestation, and the date of the accident.

I made a chronology of the photos, starting with the ones Mum took at the picnic before our accident, then the CT scans on the night of the accident, then the bruise photos, and then the self-portraits. In that sequence, it was as though the accident turned me inside out, and then right way out again.

•

I was making small excursions out into the world, but everything felt other-worldly. I wondered at people in the supermarket—'These are the ones who survived,' I thought. For all these people walking around, how many babies were there who didn't make it? I was incredulous at all this rude life in front of me. The sight of sleeping babies made me panic. How did the parents calmly pushing a pram know whether their child was still breathing? Could I see the little chest rise and fall?

Friends lent us a car, and Mum drove us around to our many appointments—GPs, hospital, counselling. I had wanted to take public transport but was told the risk of a fall (and of more internal bleeding) was too high. I was getting used to cars again, angling my broken knee across the back seat, holding onto the door handle of the taxis I took to and from rehab. But getting into the car with Rima, Jac and Jaz for the first time, to go to a movie, my slow-earned composure was suddenly gone. The sight of my legs in front of me, my feet in the same Birkenstocks I'd worn at the time of the accident, made my mouth twist into unfamiliar shapes.

'Hannah.'

My chest was heaving and it was hard to place Rima's voice.

'Hannah. You're freaking the girls out. Stop it.'

Rima's voice and her hand on my leg brought me back, and somehow I caught up with my own racing breath.

•

I was doing my physio exercises one day when the door slowly swung open, ghostlike.

'Hello?'

No one answered, but a moment later the cat slunk in. He was cautious in this part of the house. Until very recently, he'd been confined to the laundry, so he could acclimatise slowly.

Like the cat, I was gently sniffing out the expanding boundaries of my grief. At first, grief (and my bodily injuries) confined me to a white bed, then to a room, then a hospital corridor. Now the doors had all been opened and I was still cautious about where I set down each paw—wary of outside spaces and terrified of running into the territory of someone else's grief. Besides, I still had so many tender spots to investigate right here: cupboards to stick my whiskers into, beds to slink under, suitcases to peer into. The boxes of baby things that had come down with all our Sydney belongings had been repacked, into the furthest reaches of the shed.

In my dreams, cars claimed more people I loved. My best friend and her husband, crossing the road. It was sunset, and the western sun blinding. Birds swooped and confused the driver. I couldn't stop it happening, no matter how much I screamed. I dreamt I stood on a crowded platform and as I was trying to get on the train, a woman came up and whispered in my ear, 'Excuse me, are you forty-one weeks pregnant?' I shook with anger and sobs, and recited my line, 'I'm not pregnant anymore.' I dreamt that I birthed Z naturally but she slipped out and hit the floor. No one was there to catch her. And she was as white and unmoving as when I'd last seen her. I woke up weeping. When I looked over at the clock, it was 4 a.m. again, the time she was born. She and I, both cut from the wreckage.

The 'born alive' rule

In that time between coming home from rehab and the memorial, we hovered. I hummed Dusty Springfield—I didn't know what to do with myself. Some mornings were harder than others. After a particularly bad night, I took a photo of myself with each item of clothing I took off, casting off the nightmares and capturing the now yellow-greenish bruises, before a long, weepy shower. As I dressed, I took another photo for each item I put on, layering myself against the day. I imagined flicking through the photos, a jerky stop-motion film, or a nature documentary of a snake shedding its skin.

The newspaper was not quite a highlight of the day, but it was evidence that time was moving, that each new day was, apparently, distinct from the previous one. One Monday, we again found ourselves the subject of a newspaper article. Our case was one of two road accidents in Victoria that summer where a baby in utero had died. The other woman had lost not just her child in utero but also her partner. I thought of her every time I held Rima tight.

Our cases had reignited debate about the criminal law's response. Australian law followed the UK common law approach, in that criminal charges could only be laid regarding a 'death' if the person had been 'born alive'. Birth, therefore, was the moment when a legal person came into existence. Harm incurred to a fetus in utero could sometimes give rise to criminal or civil liability, but only where the baby had been born alive. This meant that, for me and for the woman who lost both her partner and her baby that summer, the charge of dangerous driving causing death could not apply because neither of our babies had shown signs of life when they were born. I had vague memories from law school of debriefing over coffee with friends after a criminal law lecture on the 'born alive' rule. But the Hannah who had sat through the lecture and could discuss death and birth in the abstract now felt as remote as a minor character in a book.

When I looked up the cases, they were grisly. In a key UK case, for example, Mr B had stabbed his partner, Ms M, with a long-bladed kitchen knife when she was around twenty-four weeks pregnant.

The knife penetrated her uterus and nicked the fetus. Ms M survived the attack, had surgery to repair her wounds and was discharged from hospital, still pregnant, and with the fetal heart making its reassuring swishy beat. But seventeen days after the attack, she went into premature labour and her daughter, S, was born, 'grossly premature'. Baby S had surgery to repair the knife wound to her abdomen and lived 121 days before dying of bronchopulmonary dysplasia. There was no evidence that the knife wound contributed to her death. Rather, she died as a result of her premature birth, which in turn was caused by the injuries inflicted on her mother when Mr B stabbed her.

Mr B was convicted of wounding Ms M with intent to cause grievous bodily harm, and after S died, was charged with murder. The matter was appealed all the way to the House of Lords, which held that 'a foetus was neither a distinct person separate from its mother nor merely an adjunct of the mother, but was a unique organism'.[1] In these circumstances, this meant that a murder conviction could not be sustained, but that Mr B could be guilty of manslaughter on the basis that his act in stabbing Ms M was 'both unlawful and dangerous because it was likely to cause harm to some person' and that it had caused the death of S.[2] Had S been stillborn instead, however, the 'born alive' rule meant that the only criminal charge would have been for causing grievous bodily harm to Ms M.

The newspaper article pictured Nancy Asani, standing (bravely, I thought, given the circumstances) in front of a car. Nancy's story was horribly familiar. In 1999, she was thirty-seven weeks pregnant (also with a little daughter) when someone driving without his headlights on ploughed onto the wrong side of the road and into her car, injuring her and killing her baby. A ripple of feeling went through me—anguish that anyone else should have been through what we were going through, but also a weird relief, of knowing that we were not the only ones. I was torn between wanting to find Nancy, so I could give her enormous, weepy hugs, and throwing the article in the bin, so I didn't have to think about it.

The 'born alive' rule

At the time of Nancy's accident, there were two possible driving offences: culpable driving causing death, which carried a sentence of up to twenty years, and dangerous driving, a charge under the *Road Safety Act*, which carried only a maximum two-year term. Because Nancy's baby, Meriem, was not born alive, the driver who caused the accident could only be convicted of dangerous driving in relation to the injury to Nancy, and was given a twelve-month sentence, two-year suspension of his licence and a $2500 fine.[3] Since then, Nancy had been campaigning for law reform.

And, in fact, the law had changed since she'd lost Meriem. Legislation in 2004 had created a new offence of dangerous driving causing serious injury or death, which was designed to fill the 'gap' between culpable and dangerous driving, and carried a maximum term of five years prison. Then, in 2008, the same legislation that took abortion out of the *Crimes Act* also clarified the definition of 'serious injury' to include 'the destruction, other than in the course of a medical procedure, of the fetus of a pregnant woman, whether or not the woman suffers any other harm'.[4]

This amendment made the Victorian legislation consistent with the law in New South Wales, where the parliament had followed the lead of the Court of Criminal Appeal in the case of *R v King*.[5] In 2002, Phillip King had discovered that Kylie Flick, the young woman he'd had a sexual encounter with, was pregnant. He was unable to convince her to terminate the pregnancy, and had allegedly offered friends $500 to punch her in the stomach, but with no takers. In August 2002, when Flick was six months pregnant, and was moving house, King contacted her, saying he wanted to 'say goodbye to her before she moved'.[6] He came over to her place, and Flick's evidence was that they spoke for about an hour, before 'everything went silent, she heard a rushing noise and as she turned she felt pressure hit her stomach'.[7] Flick testified that King punched her to the ground, then stomped on her stomach 'six or seven times'.[8]

In King's evidence, he recounted that he had been angry with Flick for threatening to tell his girlfriend about the pregnancy, but the trigger for the attack was Flick's action in lighting up a cigarette:

Q. Did you intentionally aim for her belly?
A. I wasn't—at the time I wasn't thinking, I just—everything, we were talking—everything was fine, then after—
Q. Everything was fine was it?
A. We were talking—we were talking about things and then—then things got brought up about she was going to tell my girlfriend and then I seen her light up a smoke and … then I just lost it and punched her in the stomach, she fell over and then I stomped on her right arm.
 …
Q. So you cannot be any clearer about why it was that you punched her in the stomach?
A. After that she lit up a smoke, I just—
Q. And did the cigarette smoking enrage you did it?
A. That and other things she was saying to me.
Q. Because you were concerned that it was going to damage her baby?
A. Yes.
Q. And you went along and damaged her baby instead?
A. Yes but I just—it just happened, it's not like I—I just clicked and done it, I didn't have any—yes that is.[9]

I had to read that part of the judgment several times, just to make sure I hadn't read it incorrectly. When I'd been pregnant, I'd joked with other women about the death stares you sometimes got if you were seen holding a glass of something alcoholic. But here was a direct line between the notion that pregnant women were to be policed—that their bodies were open for public judgement and advice—and a savage act of violence.

Flick was taken immediately to Bankstown Hospital, but no fetal heartbeat could be found, and her son was stillborn several days later. King was charged with maliciously inflicting grievous bodily harm with intent to do grievous bodily harm. A district court judge, however, ordered a permanent stay on the charges because she found that the Crown 'could never prove that the demise of the fetus itself and/or the abruption of the placenta amounted to grievous bodily harm to the complainant Kylie Flick' because a fetus was a 'unique organism' and therefore not part of the mother.[10] The Criminal Court of Appeal overturned this decision, with Chief Justice Spigelman finding that:

> The close physical bond between the mother and the fetus is of such a character that, for purposes of offences such as this, the fetus should be regarded as part of the mother.[11]

The 2008 Victorian *Crimes Act* amendments also split 'dangerous driving causing death or serious injury' into two distinct offences—one for death (a maximum ten-year sentence) and one for serious injury (a maximum five-year sentence). Yet, for Nancy, 'serious injury' couldn't quite sum up the enormity of her loss, and she was lobbying for something more: something 'to cover the death of unborn babies on the road'.[12] She had a point—losing Zainab was qualitatively different from suffering internal bleeding—but I was hesitant about any proposed law that was directed at a baby in utero without addressing how it might affect the person in possession of the uterus. Aside from telling Nancy's story, the article quoted various legal experts, alongside the 'Australian Family Association', a conservative lobby group that sought to exclude us, and any other families that didn't feature a husband and wife, from the definition of 'family':

> Australian Family Association spokesman John Morrissey said the inconsistencies in the state's laws appeared to exist because of 'fairly permissive abortion laws'. He supported a new law to cover the death of unborn babies in road collisions. 'An unborn baby, we all know, is no different really from a baby who was delivered maybe two days later and equipped with a birth certificate. It's nonsense to distinguish between the two,' he said.[13]

I was incensed. Not only did Mr Morrissey reduce the pregnant woman surrounding any 'unborn baby' to 'a nonsense', but he had the nerve to set this up as an either/or choice for women. Either we can access safe, legal abortion, or we can have the law recognise the harm caused when someone else's violence or carelessness ends a pregnancy, but not both. I sat down and wrote my second letter to the editor that month.

Wednesday, 27 January 2010

One month ago (though it feels like another lifetime ago), I was 34 weeks pregnant and was driving home with my family. A four-wheel drive hit us head-on, and (among our other injuries) caused my placenta to abrupt and killed my little daughter before she was born. I was so sad to read ('Mother vows to fight on for law change over road death of unborn child' *The Age* 25 Jan 2010) that Nancy Asani suffered a similar loss in December 1999, and that another woman also lost her baby this 'holiday' period.

We would support Nancy in her campaign to have the law changed to recognise that dangerous driving causing the death of an unborn baby is not just an injury to the mother. It was an injury to me, but in a much more profound way than my other injuries. Our baby, had she been delivered before the accident, would have had excellent prospects of survival—she was already 2.5kg (around 5lbs) and 48cm long. I can't put into words what we have lost and what she has lost.

What I find offensive is that anyone could try and twist our tragedy into some kind of argument against safe, legal abortion. John Morrissey, spokesman for the 'Australian Family Association', has done this in your article on Monday. How dare he try to appropriate our loss and turn it to his own political/religious ends. We were lucky not to be in a position where we had to consider abortion, but I have had a number of friends who have been in that awful position, and it is not something any woman considers lightly. Women are not stupid—we know that pregnancy is the process of turning a potential life into a living breathing child. That is what makes our loss so heartbreaking. To try and draw some connection between abortion laws and recognition of my and Nancy's loss as a loss of life is offensive and ignorant.

Hannah Robert, Preston

The newspaper published my letter, but edited it slightly, replacing 'my little daughter while she was still in utero' with 'my unborn daughter'. Nine characters rather than forty-seven. I could see the logic, but I had deliberately avoided using the word 'unborn' for Z. 'Unborn' sounded like a horror movie, *Return of the Undead*. It was a looking-glass word—the opposite of 'born', but creepier. And it was incorrect. She had been born, just not while she was alive. She wasn't un-anything. 'Unborn' sounded like a train cancellation, an almost-something, a hypothetical loss; as though you could just press the 'rewind' button and become magically unpregnant. I preferred 'dead' because it was solid, it had a weight like her two-and-a-half kilos in my arms. I knew the legal technicalities, but they were just that, about as relevant to my grief as the lot number of a land title was to the home where we lived.

'Unborn' was a grisly image on an anti-abortion protester's poster; it was an intractably polarised moral debate; it was a word I could not reconcile with my beautiful, whole, soft-cheeked daughter. I knew what my views on that debate were. Even when I'd been pregnant and in wonder at the life within me, I knew the difficult decisions that came with this amazing potential could only properly be made by the person whose body contained it. That decision—to continue or to end a pregnancy—was both a medical one about your own body and a fundamental parenting one about the quality of life you could give your potential child. I wasn't about to be forced to trade my basic beliefs about equality and autonomy for the right to grieve my child. That our loss could be churned into political capital by people who sought to impose their moral or religious views on women facing extraordinarily difficult decisions about their pregnancies made me feel sick.

I'd started seeing a psychologist at the Royal Women's Hospital, next door to the hospital where I'd spent those long days in emergency, ICU and the trauma ward. I mentioned to her that coming to the hospital for my appointments was upsetting. By this, I meant having to walk past the room where we'd held Z's funeral, and the cafeteria where we'd sat afterwards. But she gave it a very different spin.

'I know; it is hard. Did you know, there are more pregnancies terminated in this hospital than there are babies born? All those people aborting when you've just lost your child. I can imagine that is very hard.'

I was too stunned to reply on the spot. It hadn't occurred to me to begrudge others the ability to end a pregnancy for whatever reason they saw fit. I didn't want *their* pregnancies or the babies that might have resulted—that was their business. I missed *my* baby. The value I placed on her was not that she could be categorised as a fetus of a particular gestation. She was not a generic fetus, she was our daughter, and it was our relationship with *her* specifically that I grieved. Had things gone differently, who knows what decisions we might have had to make, even though she was a desperately loved and wanted baby. That love and longing to hold her in our arms did not cancel out my concern for my own (and other women's) bodily autonomy. I had started to connect online with other women grieving their babies. One had needed a second-trimester termination to prevent pre-eclampsia from taking her life; another had taken the decision to still her baby's heart in utero in the third trimester after learning that he had a condition that made him 'incompatible with life'. These were pregnancy decisions with no happy options, but they belonged unquestionably with the pregnant person, informed and supported but not dictated by medical advisers, partners and loved ones.

The 'born alive' rule

•

On a Thursday afternoon four weeks post-accident, a few days after I'd been released from hospital, we were sitting on the front porch behind the rose bushes when the postie came. This was as public as I could handle being at that time, with a thick row of thorny bushes between me and anyone I didn't know. Rima collected the mail straight away. This was about the only time in our lives together we'd actually both been home on a weekday to see the postman. Among the mail was a post-pack with six CDs of images from the Royal Melbourne radiology department.

We loaded up the first one ('CT–Trauma series 1/3') and were told it had 2166 images on it. We didn't get past the first image. It showed my body, from my neck down to about my shins, with my arms held above my head.

I remembered this being taken. It hurt so much to lie like that, and you could see the pain in the awkward, lopsided way I was lying to try not to put pressure on the sorest, most broken bits of my body. The time on the image was '20:26'. It was after I'd found out that Haloumi had died, but before they had operated to take her out and to repair my knee. And you could see her there, curled within me. To my un-medically trained eye, she looked for all the world like a beautiful, healthy living baby. My flesh and hers looked the same—how could mine be living and hers not?

That Thursday night, I had so many dreams it was hard to believe they could all fit into one night. But, best and hardest of all, Z visited me in my dreams. I was on the CountryLink train to Newcastle and she lay on the tray table before me; as cold and still as when I'd last seen her. I was watching over her. I had to get her safely to her destination, but the sun coming through the window was warm and the lull of the train moving made my eyelids heavy. I realised with a shock that I'd fallen asleep and guilt shot through me for breaking my vigil. But as I awoke, her eyelids fluttered open, just as mine had. I embraced her and wept,

You're alive! Oh, my little love, my little one! This time, constant waves of baby expressions animated her face. She looked directly at me and I heard her say, in an adult voice, *Are you okay?* Before I could reassure her, I was waking up again, this time for real.

11
Sun salute with bedpan

The hardest and the best bit for me about yoga is when you are doing something difficult, when it feels like your bones just cannot move the way you're asking them to. It's uncomfortable and your initial reaction is *No—enough; I can't do this*. But then you notice the discomfort, acknowledge it, breathe in, and then, as you breathe out, move past it. You ask an open question of your body, and sometimes it responds in surprising ways. Things unfold, settle, stretch. And you realise that the thing you had thought was unimaginably difficult … well, you've already been doing it for thirty seconds. The answer was there all along, within you; you just needed to ask the right question, and to listen patiently for an answer. It doesn't happen all the time, but when it does, it is good. It restores my faith, it reminds me that sometimes my body knows more than my mind.

When I'd still been in the trauma ward, I had been desperate to move my creaky body, all gummed up with bruises. What I really wanted to do was yoga—some kind of yoga that was possible with my broken bones and wounds.

I left a long, garbled phone message for a woman in the physiotherapy unit at Royal Prince Alfred Hospital, where I had attended a yoga session only a few weeks before we left Sydney. This wasn't the usual yoga environment, with candles, pictures of lotus flowers or other hippy accoutrements. There was hospital carpet, a sensible colour scheme; it was institutional, rather than inspirational, décor. I hadn't been to this class before and didn't know anyone, so I shrank into myself a little. The room was packed with very pregnant women, all taking up more space than they were used to, and with no non-pregnant people to make room for them. So entrenched was I in solitary mode that it took me a moment to realise I did in fact know someone—an old friend—and that she was waving at me.

'Hello, Renee!'

'Hannah!'

We hugged, making an awkward A shape over two big bellies. 'When are you due?' she asked.

'February! How about you?'

'January! And you know Karin is pregnant too? Due in December.'

'No, I didn't know. That is hilarious! Three in three months. Are they still in Paris?'

'Yes, having a little French *bébé*! Um, we'd better …' The instructor, an older woman with a loose grey bun, had come in and class was about to start, so we found our places and smiled at one another in a 'Let's talk later' way.

•

The RPA instructor didn't get back to me, so it wasn't until I'd been released from rehab that I ventured out to a yoga class. I'd spoken on the phone with the owner of the studio, as I needed to deal with someone who understood the backstory. Penny and my sister came with me, flanking me as I, with my crutches, worked my creaky way up the long staircase to the yoga studio.

•

Sun salute with bedpan

Yoga was my answer to my official rehabilitation plan, which mostly involved taking Panadeine Forte and screaming into a pillow while the physio put his body weight into forcing my knee to bend. Afterwards, he would measure the new degree of flexion with a giant Perspex protractor as though I were a Year Nine maths project.

'Why does it hurt this much?' I asked him.

'Your knee was healing straight for three weeks, so we need to break down a whole lot of scar tissue in the joint.'

'And when you say "break down", do you mean tear it? Because that's what it feels like.'

'I guess so. But it has to happen if you want your full range of motion again.'

He was a nice enough bloke, but I hated him for his casualness, for the fact that he didn't take my pain personally, and that he was more concerned with refining the details of the TAC paperwork than with my suffering.

•

Before the yoga class began, the teacher approached us, noticing that we were new.

'Hi, I'm Jess,' she smiled.

I explained that I'd called in advance to say that my knee could only bend so far, that I was also recovering from a C-section, that our baby died. It is hard to remember that first conversation with Jess without the overlay of all my subsequent conversations with her, and all her gently worded yoga instructions. But I know that she contained her shock, that she didn't do the 'tragedy recoil' that so many people unconsciously do. And after offering her condolences, she smiled—not to trivialise what I'd just told her, but as pure kindness; as a reassurance that she would watch out for me, that this was a good place to be, even if I came here broken.

•

At home, in our new bedroom, I laid out my yoga mat, and stood, feet hip-width apart. I flexed my toes, spread them as wide as I could and, from little toe to big, re-placed them on the mat. *Breathe in*, hands to heart; then, breathing out, I swung my right leg back behind me, making a broad-based triangle. No, nothing was really triangle-shaped. I was rusty and bruised, still regaining sovereignty over the remodelled territory of my body. My body facing to the side, I raised my arms to stretch out my hands to either horizon, and turned my head to face my left hand. I breathed in; and then, with the out-breath, I bent that once-broken knee as close to ninety degrees as I could, and focused my gaze along the middle finger of my left hand, like a magic laser beam. *Warrior Two.* Rima and my mum stood in the doorway and cheered. My gaze took a direct line, into space and into the path of a hurtling silver four-wheel drive. *Bring it on, universe—if you want to mess with me, I will take you on.*

12

The posthumous godfather

Thursday, 21 January 2010

Dear Joan,

I hope this finds you and the rest of your family well. I've been thinking of you often since David's funeral, but particularly in the last three and a half weeks. Three and a half weeks ago something awful happened—while I don't want to distress you, I feel like I need to tell you because I have an odd request to make of you. If it is too much, please just let this letter go by the by and I promise never to pester you again, and apologise for pestering in the first place. But grief is a strange thing which can make you behave quite oddly, so I feel compelled to write on the off-chance that you don't mind.

Three and a half weeks ago I was involved in a serious car accident. I had been driving to my dad's house with my partner Rima (who you met briefly at David's funeral) and two of Rima's daughters (my stepdaughters) in the car. I was 34 weeks pregnant—with a baby we had been planning and trying for for about four years via assisted conception.

Four of us survived the crash, but our baby did not. We were sent to three different hospitals—all injured but thankfully with no serious brain or spinal injuries. We are still recovering now, and will be for some time. I am writing because in the days after our little daughter died, the thought which was driving me mad with grief was the thought of her being alone—crying and not understanding why we were not there to comfort her. No baby should be alone and uncared for.

And then, after I thought my heart would burst with tears, a little comforting thought came to me. I thought, this is why parents give their children godparents—to care for their child when they are not able to. And that, wherever our baby is, we would need to find godparents in that place to hold her and to explain to her how much we love her and how badly we wished we could care for her ourselves, but that a terrible thing had happened—not her fault and not our fault—which had stranded us in different worlds.

So we needed to think of godparents who were in the same place as our little girl. We first thought of Rima's cousin, who was like a brother to Rima, and passed away very suddenly in April 2008. We also thought about a dear family friend of mine in the UK, who had died of breast cancer nearly two years ago, and who had been like a mother to me at several times in my life when I really needed her.

And I thought of course of David. Because David really was more like a godparent than a mentor to me in his generosity with his time, energy and guidance. He shaped my teaching, my research and my writing more than I realised at the time, but was also incredibly supportive in his personal capacity.

I imagine he might make a slightly gruff, but very loving and extremely knowledgeable and protective godfather for our daughter. We would be honoured if you felt able to give your consent as earthly guardian of David's memory.

I'm not sure what your beliefs are on what happens after death, so I sincerely hope this request is not an offensive one. Up until now I'd had the luxury of never having to think too hard about it. I'm still quite fuzzy about it but I realise I do believe that souls go somewhere, and

The posthumous godfather

that where that somewhere is really doesn't have too much to do with what religion the person has followed during their life. I really hope that this is the case, because the three people we would like to have as Z's godparents are each of different faiths—Ahmed Muslim, Rosie Christian and David Jewish. If this godparent arrangement 'works', at the very least she will be well educated in the religions of the book!

My partner Rima has similar beliefs to mine, but within the framework of the faith she was raised within—Islam. It was very important to her that our child be Muslim (at least until she could make a decision for herself) so we have given her Muslim rites and an Arabic name.

This is all a lot to take in. Please have a think about our request—if there is any more information you need to know please let me know. Or, if it is easier, you may wish to talk with Rosalind (who also came and spoke at David's funeral).

We are having a multi-faith memorial service for our little girl on Sunday, 7 February down at Somers on the Mornington Peninsula. We have included an invitation and you would be very welcome, but please don't feel obliged to come. I realise interstate travel is expensive and disrupting. If you are happy for us to nominate David as a godparent, we will include something brief in the ceremony to this effect. We're not sure how cryptic we will be about it—the whole concept (as you can see from this letter) takes a bit of explaining.

If you could let us know either way before the 7th of February— either directly or via Rosalind—that would be much appreciated.

With love and the fondest of memories of David,

Hannah

•

Prior to our accident, my longest stay in hospital had been as a seven year old. I'd always complained of 'tummy aches', but the winter my baby sister was born, the tummy aches got worse, and were eventually diagnosed as recurrent kidney infections. My mum realised that this wasn't an ordinary tummy ache when I couldn't leave the couch, squirming and weeping with the pain. Even the novelty of having a doctor come to our house was only a minor distraction from the dull but intense ache in my side. Once the kidney infection was diagnosed and being treated, I underwent an unpleasant test involving a catheter, an isotope and an X-ray machine, and it was revealed I had a congenital defect. The ureter on my right side was misplaced, and was allowing urine to flow back up to the kidney; hence the recurrent infections and damage to that part of the kidney. I was going to need an operation to correct the ureter and to remove the damaged part.

At seven, I was delighted by this news. In primary-school currency, a broken arm or leg brought instant popularity; the thought of hospital and an Operation (just like the 1980s electric board game!) made my small mind explode with the possibilities. Indeed, when the Operation was delayed a week, I turned up to school, and everyone was making get-well-soon cards for me and hastily had to hide them away. I still have the photo of all those cards Blu-tacked around my hospital bed, with me grinning smugly in my new pyjamas in the middle of them all, clutching my Care Bear—another hospital trophy.

It was in that hospital bed that I learned to read properly. Not to spell out letters or say the words; I'd learned how to do that at school. But to read—to breathe in a story, to weave your own dreams from its dangling threads, to leap wholeheartedly and without realising you've leapt into another person's world. At the start of my week in hospital, my parents took turns reading to me; by the end of the week, I was reading to them.

The book was *The Brothers Lionheart* by Astrid Lindgren—it still rates as one of my favourite books of all time. It didn't strike me until recently that perhaps a book that starts with two little boys dying might be considered morose reading for a seven year old in hospital. But it wasn't morose, not in the least, because dying was just the kicking-off point for marvellous adventures for these kids, in a world where they

The posthumous godfather

could fight dragons, and lead revolutions, and learn that sometimes, even people you loved failed you. This wasn't 'heaven' and it certainly wasn't a cushy affair with clouds, harps and eternal life. In my pink pyjamas and with my seven-year-old certainty, I wasn't scared of dying, and I didn't find out until years later what a close thing it had been, for a moment there. But when my grandparents died, I thought of them as there, in Astrid Lindgren's Nangijala, going on with their slightly more adventurous lives and sending us a dove every now and then.

I hit a snag, though, in another hospital room twenty-six years later, when the buzz of medical people doing things to various remote parts of me had stopped at last, and I was left alone, and with-it enough, to think for the first time since the accident. My belly was still so swollen, but not with Z—so where was she? We'd just farewelled her cold little face, so where was my moving, hiccuping baby? What exactly did I believe happened after death? Rubber, meet Road.

I'd been to Sunday school and to church with my parents for a short period, but none of it rang true for me. If I had to sit through a Christian service, I would find myself going in argumentative circles in my head. So if I couldn't bring myself to believe in heaven or hell, could I believe in Nangijala? Another life, just as mortal and complex as our own, with some familiar characters but different props? It seemed to work okay for my grandparents, but what about Z? She was too small for adventures, too small for riding horses and fighting dragons. She was still too small to be away from me and my heartbeat, or even to know how the whole communication-via-doves thing works. If small babies have trouble knowing that their parents still exist when they play peek-a-boo, then what hope did Z have of knowing how much we loved her, stranded as she was from us by death?

All I could think of was her wailing, in a rustic-looking basket on someone's stone doorstep, and her little hands searching, and rustling the swaddling clothes. Someone would come, of course, but who? Some anonymous pre-modern wet nurse? I couldn't work out which was worse—to think of her annihilated and stopped forever, or to think of her continuing on without us, lost and disconnected. Both scenarios made me howl and choke.

This was why I had to invent the idea of godparents, to populate her imaginary world with people we loved, who knew us and who could tell her how much we loved her, who could sort out doves for her. It kind of worked, but it still felt like an invention, a delusion to make things feel okay. And it still tore my heart to imagine her crying, and not being able to pick her up.

The week after I had been released from rehab, I sat down to write my rather odd letter to Joan Philips, the mother of the late David Philips, who had supervised my master's thesis, and who had employed me in the history department for four years as a sessional tutor while I was finishing my MA and law degree. David was South African. After doing his first degree, at the University of Witwatersrand, he'd won a Rhodes Scholarship to study for his PhD at Oxford. He was passionately involved in the anti-apartheid movement and decided he did not want to return to South Africa while that regime prevailed. So he took a job at the University of Melbourne, where (a couple of decades on) I encountered him in a first-year subject on comparative colonial history. He was an imposing man—an associate professor by that stage—and he unapologetically took up space both physically and intellectually, and demanded that you, in turn, stand your ground and explain your position. He was fierce, but funny and good hearted. In a year when I was heartbroken from breaking up with my first girlfriend, David and my co-supervisor, Pat Grimshaw, helped me refocus on the thesis and get it written.

In August 2008, David had just retired, and was on holiday in Broome, when he died suddenly of a heart attack. Rosalind Hearder, a friend and colleague who'd taught with David and me, called. I was delighted to hear from her, but when I heard her tone, my heart dropped. It hadn't occurred to me that David wouldn't be here forever, and there were so many things I'd neglected to tell him. Rosalind and I asked David's family if we could attend his funeral, and offered to say

The posthumous godfather

something on behalf of his students and university colleagues. David's mother, Joan, welcomed us, and so we went along to the funeral, and spoke briefly about David and his significant impact on our lives and the lives of his students and colleagues.

Eighteen months later, the January after our accident, I was thinking a lot about David. He appeared in one of my dreams, in the crowds outside Shea Stadium in New York, which we'd visited in the months after he died. I was shocked to see him and said, 'David, I thought you were dead.' He guffawed at the idea and said, in his characteristic style, 'Hannah, you are clearly incorrect!'

Joan wrote back, giving her blessing for us to appoint David as a posthumous godfather to our daughter, and recommending we go see the movie *Invictus*, which she thought he would have loved. The night before the memorial, I dug through the filing cabinet in the garage to find a page with his handwriting on it—the first page of the final draft of my master's thesis. Seeing his lead-pencil handwriting, I blinked. I could see his office; I'd always have to move a pile of books so I could lean my notepad on the desk to take notes during our meetings.

We took the page with us to Somers. There, my dad folded it into a paper aeroplane and gave it several maiden flights before the service, when we buried it with Z's ashes.

•

For a while after the memorial, the sadness made me paper-thin. Just breathing, opening my eyes and looking at my surviving loved ones felt so hard. I was glad of the automatic breathing reflex, because I certainly couldn't have bothered doing it consciously. The rich smell of lillies pervaded our house. Not everyone had got the 'no flowers, just donate to Oxfam' memo, and I couldn't just throw them out. They were beautiful. They were tangible expressions of love and sorrow. But watching them open, spill their pollen and slowly die, was less heart-warming. Still life, indeed. We'd had enough of that.

The memorial was hard but good—in a painfully satisfying way. We felt so loved, by everyone who came, and by everyone who didn't come but sent messages or cards. It felt strangely like a wedding (perhaps because my dad and stepmum got married there nearly twelve years before), except for the volume of the weeping. We may not have been allowed our own wedding in this country, but Rima and I were now wedded in this grief.

An hour before the service started, I left things in everyone else's hands and hobbled off to the beach with Rima, my sister and my brother. Jez and I went in the water—him rapidly, like an otter (his stubbly beard adding to the otter impression), and me slowly, letting the water lap its way up my broken body. It was warmer than usual, crystal clear and with very little seaweed.

I dived down and opened my eyes, feeling for the bottom with my hands. I came up, rolled onto my back and let myself float. How many days and hours since I last did that—but in the ocean baths in Sydney, and with Haloumi also floating inside me? And I thought of the spectacle I presented then, with my belly popping above the water like a fleshy island. The girls had thought it was hilarious when I took them to the pool and did backstroke; my belly sinking and rising with each stroke.

Now my fleshy island was just a wrinkly belly below the surface. I sobbed and let my tears mingle with the big, salty sorrow of the sea.

And, as always happens when I float like that, I realised that I'd stopped being aware of time, and was startled back into myself. When I opened my eyes and rolled over, Jez was floating right there beside me.

Somehow, time disappeared and, although we'd arrived about two hours early, we didn't get a chance to test the music system, with the result that none of the music played properly. We would get the first few stanzas, and then it flickered in and out and was awful to hear. The songs I'd listened to on repeat in the hospital, which had come to feel as if they were written about us and our loss, were reduced to

The posthumous godfather

crackling static and snatches of a tune. I was cranky about it, but Rima was philosophical and calmed me with little pats on the arm.

Afterwards, we dried our salty cheeks as we walked back from the bush chapel, and ate and laughed and hugged people we hadn't seen for months. I had made platters and platters of haloumi and zucchini fritters. The zucchinis had gone crazy in the vegie patch we'd inherited from our tenants. A friend had asked, half-seriously, while I was still in hospital, 'Does this mean you can never eat haloumi again? Because it will be kind of like eating her?'

'No, no,' I'd chided. 'We will eat it in remembrance of her!'

The next day, there were plates of the remaining haloumi zucchini fritters in the fridge. I didn't want to throw them out; doing so felt sacrilegious. Our friends and family had gone home with full bellies and sore eyes, and now this leftover grief was ours to continue eating, day after day, magically renewed every time we finished it, like a weepy magical pudding.

An old friend who lived interstate called—could she come and visit? Was it okay if she brought her baby daughter?

People had been extra thoughtful about not bringing babies into our presence, as though I might be allergic to them. 'No, please bring her. That would be lovely.'

She did, and the minute she walked in the door, asked, 'Do you want to hold her?' I did, and we looked at the pictures of Z and talked, while fat tears dropped onto her baby's wispy head.

13

Matryoshka

On the one-month anniversary of the accident, Rima and I were at the doctor's again. Our GP, Kelvin, was our new best friend in Melbourne. We'd picked an inner-suburban clinic that friends had recommended as LGBTI-friendly. None of the lesbian doctors we asked about were taking on new patients, so we reluctantly made an appointment with one of the male doctors. I presumed that he'd be expert on sexual health and drug interactions, but perhaps not so comfortable dealing with 'women's issues'—and we had plenty of those.

At the first appointment, though, Kelvin didn't bat an eyelid. He sat and listened as we gave him the matter-of-fact version of the accident, paying compassionate attention, but not reacting. Then he offered help with the pragmatics of referrals, prescriptions and insurance certificates. He quickly became expert at summing up our story in a sentence or less; and navigating the bureaucracy of the three hospitals we'd had to deal with, as well as the government insurer who covered all vehicle accidents. This time, he was on the phone to the histopathology department at Royal Melbourne, on the Trail of the Disappearing Placenta.

Not much of Z's birth had gone to plan, but the one request the midwives had thought they could help with was to keep Z's placenta, so that we could bury it under a tree. A tree with a transient body part buried under it was a lousy substitute for a daughter, but it was something. Or it would have been, if only we could convince the histopathologist to give us back the placenta.

While Kelvin was on the phone, Rima found a set of nested matryoshka dolls in the toy basket. She looked at me, opened the first doll, and made her goofy 'Surprise!' face as she pulled out the next doll, making me smile. She opened the next and the next. There was surprise all the way down, until, 'Ohhhhh'—sad face—when the last, tiniest doll could not open. The last of the line. My silent giggle turned into a sad face too, and I thought, 'I don't want to be that doll.'

On my next trip to the doctor, I discovered a hobby shop within hobbling-on-crutches distance, and bought several slabs of balsa wood and a small set of tools, so I could start whittling my own morose matryoshka set. The first and biggest doll was not a doll at all, but our car post impact, the front driver's corner crushed in. Our car had been a Nimbus, a puffy little white cloud of a station wagon with Tardis-like properties. I hollowed out four spots inside, for Rima, Jac, Jas and me, and made small dolls for each of us. And then I hollowed out my own rounded doll, and made a tiny one to fit inside. It was harder than I'd thought. My whittling skills were pretty ordinary and the balsa did not behave as I expected it to. It was probably the wrong kind of wood. But there it was—a chunky wooden approximation of our wrecked car, with us wrecked inside it, and our daughter, the most terminally wrecked of all, inside me.

I made a little black-bordered birth announcement card, with an open matryoshka doll in one corner, the two empty halves leaning against one another. She had a sweepy fringe like mine and a chubby tear rolling down her cheek. In the opposite corner was a tightly swaddled dark-haired babushka baby, long eyelashes resting on her cheeks. A thick black border connected the two. We had the cards printed with Z's name, weight, length, date of birth and a message in the centre. I had grand plans of sending them out to all the friends and family who had visited, helped and sent us cards, flowers and love, but every time I got out the list, I only managed a few before it all just felt too, too sad.

My Aunty Connie came to see us. When I was eleven, and her son was thirteen, he killed himself with a handgun—whether by accident or not, we'll never know. She was blunt. 'Your life is split now,' she said. 'There'll always be before, and …', she sighed, '… after.' I imagined the bit in between as a gaping chasm, so that reminders of before felt like stranded relics, completely irrelevant and alien in their new setting. Not only my clothes, and our things as we gradually unpacked, but even songs on the radio. Books did not pass through my hands without me flipping to the front to find the publication date, so I could work out if it was a naïve resident of 'before', or a wiser, sadder survivor of 'after'.

Tuesday, 16 February 2010

I visited the dentist this morning to have my front teeth repaired. They'd been chipped in the accident, when my jaws banged together like a nutcracker puppet. I'm usually one of those strange people who quite likes visiting the dentist, but today, holding my mouth open and seeing the dentist work above me, I was suddenly back in the ER, clothes sliced off and my body pinned down to the spinal board like a prize butterfly in a neck brace—a disinterested observer to the workplace that was my body.

Now my teeth are dulled again—the sharpness of chipped edges no longer catching on my tongue. I feel dulled too—shell shocked. The bomb has gone off—a good seven and a half weeks ago, and I'm still stunned, staring into space.

If I were a chimpanzee in the zoo, today would be the day I would spend with a blanket on my head, occasionally hitting myself (and others, if they came near) with a small tree branch. The equivalent human behaviour is staying in bed and eating 70% cacao chocolate, while listening to 90s grunge pop. Friends have made mixtapes for us—I played these and made my own lists to include the lyrics which echoed around my head about the 'saddest summer ever' and 'help I'm alive, my heart keeps beating like a hammer'.

After the dentist, we went back to the hospital to meet with the same bow-tied obstetrician who had told us Haloumi had died. It was as though the movie was over and we were chatting with one of the actors on how the movie played out—reflecting on the motivations and plot, the 'makings of'.

I feel slowed. I still don't get it. There were women walking out of the hospital with babies tinier than mine. Living, breathing babies. Some with less hair than mine, some with more. Where is my baby? Where is she? Why can't she be here in my arms? Why can't we be fussing over her carseat so we can take her home? I know these thoughts are not productive, whatever that means. I still want to know. I was that close to having a living child in my arms.

I dreamt that I was at Z's memorial service again, but I was riding a child's ride-on toy. It was too small and whenever I stopped moving it would slide out from under me and ignominiously dump my bottom on the ground. A work colleague was there and remarked, 'Oh Hannah! So good to see you getting around!'

In another dream, I was cutting rosebuds, each with a dead rosehead in the centre. In another, I had to walk through a pool of shining wet eels, a dark slithering against my skin. Things were lost, landscapes disoriented, obstacles stood in my way. I had another baby and she lived, but I couldn't remember her date of birth. Was she Z's twin? Or had another whole pregnancy elapsed within seven weeks?

The other night I dreamt that I walked into a Victorian terrace house. A slick-looking bloke put his hands together in greeting: 'It's already started but what I'd suggest is that you join in with the group upstairs.' I could hear voices raised and chairs pushed across the floor in the room above. Before I could climb the stairs, he caught my sleeve: 'The scenario is—it is 1939 and you are requested to go on a secret mission to get sixteen European leaders to sign a pact undermining the Treaty of Warsaw, pre-empting it and giving them an out.'

It didn't make sense to me. I felt foolish—I didn't know enough to ask a meaningful question.

'The main obstacle is this Austrian bloke who wouldn't sign because he'd been circumcised.'

'Circumcised? What did that have to do with it?'

'He objects to the subterfuge. He wants it all out in the open. We need to convince him …', he looked at me meaningfully, '… that this is the only way'.

I wanted to ask why, but he's gone, and there are stairs I must climb.

It is chaos upstairs. I'm frightened. I know this is pretend, but it feels like a very serious sort of pretend.

I was still waking at 4 a.m. most nights. The sadness would ball up in my stomach so much that I wanted to throw it up, to get it out of my system so I could somehow go back to the land of 'before'. I could see now the appeal in imagining things like this as being punishment by a vengeful god. Once you are punished, the balance is levelled and you can't be punished again for it—apparently even God operates under a concept of double jeopardy. But if it's not punishment, if it's all random universal cruelty, then it could happen again at any time, and to anyone I love.

Sunday, 21 February 2010

Seven weeks. Seven times seven. 49 bare little squares between us and her last heartbeat. 49 days later I can walk, I can go to the toilet by myself, I'm even contemplating going back to work. When people told me that time would heal, I didn't realise that all this healing also takes me away from her—our ship is sailing on without her. I'm still not sure I can let go. I know she'll always follow us; no longer as a

Matryoshka

living passenger—maybe as a gull we can see from a distance, who sometimes lights on the bow. Sometimes she'll swoop in close and I'll think she's still with us, other times we might not see her for days at a time. I feel like my brain is a machine which keeps spitting out metaphors for this grief—(here I go again) one error message after another. It still does not compute.

Even her birth date and death dates feel like a mathematical error. She died on the 27th and was born on the 28th—birth and death folded in on one another so that they come in the wrong order.

My phone has mysteriously reset its own date and time to 9 a.m. on 1 January 2007. Imagine that—three and a bit years ago we were at a friends' holiday house, greeting a new year. It feels so distant, but part of me knows it wasn't an idyll. It was an ordinary life. I still have moments of that and I know the moments will come closer together with time.

14

Histopathology

When my dad had visited me in rehab, he'd brought little offerings to make me feel better: a newspaper clipping about the zoo, little sachets of miso soup, a small posy of violets. And, one day, a pomegranate. Everything about it was exquisite. Once my visitors had gone home for the day, I held it in my hand—a crimson magical orb. It felt too beautiful to cut up.

The next morning, I was just waking up when one of the catering ladies brought in my breakfast. She asked how I was and, as I struggled to get a sentence out of my pasty, still-asleep mouth, she sighted the pomegranate on the bedside table. 'This! Good antioxidants! Very good for your healing!' It was both an admonishment and a command, but kindly ones, so I was happy to comply.

I'd eaten a pomegranate before, but never dissected one like I did that day. The process of cutting into the fruit and cracking it open felt like some kind of brutal surgery, the seeds bleeding into my fingers. I peeled away chunks of pith and peel, at once leathery and delicate— football red on the outside and a soft cream on the inside. Row on honeycombed row of translucent seeds were lodged into the pith like teeth in gums, each compartment veiled from the others with a filmy rose–yellow silk membrane. I prised them out one by one, and took photos of all of it: the broken scraps of peel, the membrane, the seeds. Here was something that, even when split apart and broken, only revealed more beauty.

A few days after I was released from rehab, and could join Rima and the girls in our new house, a pomegranate tree was delivered. It was a gift, in Z's name, from dear friends who lived overseas. It stood, green and hopeful, on the porch as the summer days and weeks wore on—hot and dry. I feared it would die there. I almost willed it to die there, and then was torn by guilt at the idea that I could kill my daughter's memory in plant form. Nonetheless, we waited.

At first we were waiting for the placenta. I wanted to bury those cells that belonged to both Z and me underneath the tree. Our midwives at the hospital had dutifully saved the placenta. The histopathologists at the hospital were holding it, after having examined it to confirm the cause of Z's death. I had to look up what histopathology meant. It was from the Greek: *histos* 'tissue', *pathos* 'suffering', and *logia* 'study of'—the study of suffering tissue. The histopathologists had not met Z or me, but there they were, making a study of our suffering by examining the bloody organ that had joined us; at least, until it came unplugged.

When I tried to follow up the placenta issue, we were invited to a meeting at the hospital. The people there put on their understanding faces, and made 'Sorry for your loss' noises. The doctor seemed horrified by our predicament. The placenta had been treated with formaldehyde, making it toxic. I imagined it floating in a jar and asked, 'Does that mean you want to keep it?'

'No, no, but it has to be disposed of as medical waste. Not so great to plant in your garden, especially if you want to grow food there.' It was a very long way of saying, 'No, you can't have it.'

The doctor carefully watched us absorb this information. I wasn't sure what she was expecting; perhaps a hysterical grieving woman screaming, 'Give me back my placenta!' I was tempted, but didn't have the energy for staging a revolt this time.

There were pragmatic considerations too. If I went leaking this grief all over the place every time I was triggered, I'd be a big mess. We'd had to live with what had happened for over seven weeks now and were weary of it. It was not a surprise anymore; this was our banal, everyday horror. 'Forgive me,' I wanted to say. 'Forgive me if I don't seem as shocked and as saddened as you—the person who has just heard this awful news. Believe me, we still feel it, and there are plenty of moments when I turn a corner and bump into a new aspect of the horror and feel the shock all over again. But most of the time we have to keep a lid on it, for our own sanity. To mix metaphors, we can't keep picking at our scabs just to demonstrate our wounds.'

I remembered going to see a dear friend, F, maybe a week and a half after her brother's funeral, when we were both in second year at university. I was distraught—for her, at the thought of losing my own brother, and at the idea of death itself. Her calm surprised me, and now it made sense—that weary familiarity when you've been wearing grief for a while, so that it begins to feel normal, when you've cried all you can for the moment.

So, by that time the fight had gone out of me. The poor histopathologists; I think it was probably quite odd for them to have the owner of some tissue they had preserved and examined show up and demand it back. From then on, we were no longer waiting on medical bureaucrats but on my own battered ability to make decisions and to dig a hole.

The drought had killed a small tree in the front yard. It stood, unrepentantly ugly, between our bay window and the front fence. I didn't know what kind of tree it was. Much as I liked the idea of a garden, gardening itself was still something I thought old people did. It was nearly March by the time we started digging the tree out, when the Preston clay was at its hardest. I threw the pick at the ground, over and over again, carving out the rough outline of a circle around the dead tree. The arc of the pick swinging up, the rush down and the 'thuck' of contact, the sheer solidity of the earth, was a relief. I didn't need to weep, or think, or speak. Just dig. My convalescent limbs were sore and sweaty from the work. I took a long bath with some luxury bath powder my sister had given me for Christmas, just two days before the accident.

The next day I carried bucket after bucket of cold, milky water across the porch and out to our hole. I gave the dead tree a relaxing bath in my second-hand bathwater. The clay held the water almost as well as the enamel bathtub. The digging, to my regret, had to be postponed while the water level slowly soaked lower and lower until I braved the mud and worried away at the dead tree's root system, carving away the stiff mud. My dad and, occasionally, Rima took turns, but I was alone for the last bit, when the tree developed a tantalising wobble, like that of a loose tooth. Even then, it took nearly an hour for it to give way with a satisfying crunch, the small dead tree suddenly lurching, so that it looked more dead and more out of place than before. Remembering what it was like to feel strong in my unfamiliar, resurrected body, I lifted it partway out of the hole before calling for help.

It left a crater in the front yard; a crater I tended lovingly with clay-breaker and compost, before we finally eased the sickly looking pomegranate tree into the hole. Promptly upon arriving in its new home, the tree dropped the rest of its leaves for autumn, leaving us to wonder about its survival until spring. Miraculously, come August, there were tiny red buds. Having eschewed the colour red for autumn yellows, our little pomegranate tree wore red for spring instead.

I would prune the miniature roses at the front of the house, making a tiny posy to bring inside, and then carrying the loose petals and dead flowerheads over to the pomegranate tree. I would sprinkle the petals at the base of the tree, giving it a composting carpet of pink, red and yellow–gold–pink. It became a ritual. It was a chance to have a natter with my beautiful girl, to feel the leaves brush at the side of my face like small hands. *I miss you, my little love. I wish you were in the house, being loud.* I would kneel in the front yard, chatting to a pomegranate tree. I was okay with being the crazy grieving mother of the neighbourhood if it meant I could chat with my daughter. Or maybe they thought I was just a very attentive gardener?

15

Proof

Things are moving towards 'normal'. We are all home from hospital, I'm walking unassisted, there is talk of returning to work. One day, we grab the mail on our way out of the house to have coffee with an old friend. I tear an envelope open and can tell from the feel of the paper that it is not a bill. This is thicker, watermarked paper, like that of a bank cheque or a passport page. When I stare at it, I can't tell whether it is just my eyes or whether the colour of the paper changes softly towards the centre—from creamy white to pinky cream.

Here is my name, and Rima's; here is the name we chose for her and her date of birth. This paper certifies me as a 'mother', and certifies Z's birth; that she was here, a human child, even if she never drew breath. Part of me wonders why they produce these certificates. Is she ever going to need it to get a passport? To get her driver's licence? Will we ever need it to enrol her in school? No, this certificate is for us, to make us feel better, to offer administrative proof of our child's existence. A child was here. She must be recorded.

On paper, I am a mother, but there is no pram here; no noisy, squirming baby. I feel like one of those flat felt figures we had at kinder. You can peel me off this situation and stick me onto another. It makes a soft ripping sound as you do it, quieter than velcro. Here is my picture-baby, here is my piece of paper. I love her so much, but she's now my two-dimensional child—stilled, flattened out on the page like a rare flower. I didn't dream her three-dimensional little life, she was definitely here (*right here*), moving and being. But all the remaining evidence I have of that fact is unsatisfying.

The next envelope I open is an overdue fine from the library: *Sheila Kitzinger, Rediscovering Birth.* We have to go, to move on; we'll be late for coffee with Aron. I fold these pieces of mail together, and worry that I'll mix them up or lose them—confuse the proof of my daughter's existence with a library fine.

•

About a month after I'd been released from hospital, my dad and stepmum decided to take me to see the Melbourne Symphony Orchestra because, as my dad put it, 'music is good for the soul'. They could tell my soul needed all the help it could get. In some strange cosmic joke, the first piece was Fauré's Pavane—one of the pieces we'd played at Z's funeral. It was on a classical music CD that Rima liked to play to my pregnant tummy.

After the funeral, the CD player had stayed with me in intensive care and then in the trauma ward, and I played that CD over and over. It drowned out the sound of my weeping, and somehow the weeping felt less pathetic with a majestic orchestral backing track. There in the concert hall, shiny program on my lap, the same notes from the trauma ward came flooding back at me, live and properly oceanic. Silent tears wet my cheeks, and my dad squeezed my hand.

•

Reinstating 'normal' meant we needed to buy a new death-machine (ahem, car), and get it insured. We'd received a 'Bereavement Payment' from the government—they don't call it the 'Baby Bonus' when your baby dies. With that, and the money from the insurance payout from the old car, we could afford a much newer and safer car, with enough airbags to demand their own collective noun. A cloud of airbags? A reassurance of airbags? I was sulky about paying good money for another car when the last one had stolen our child from us. I was less angry with the human error and thoughtlessness that had caused our accident than I was with these dangerous machines, and the extent to which we were reliant on them and complacent about their propensity to kill us.

Still, in order to see family, and get to and from the shops and various medical appointments, we needed a car. Back in the trauma ward, I had made a rule for myself: that my decisions would be led by what my family and I needed to heal and recover, not by fear or shame. So, even though the thought of driving still gave me the shakes, we started shopping for a new car.

My dad took us on expeditions to inspect cars, carefully navigating so that we didn't need to travel along the road that had been the scene of our accident. We avoided the car yards full of four-wheel drives and the sense of queasy doom they gave me. And, finally, we found something—a creamy-white station wagon with plenty of airbags; auto emergency braking; and, best of all, a GPS system with a calm and reassuring voice. We called her Pearl, as though having a humanised name for our car could somehow immunise us against the risk of another accident.

Each person I spoke to as I called around getting insurance quotes had to ask whether we'd had any previous accidents in the past three years, 'regardless of fault'. I would tell them, 'Yes, we had a serious crash, just in December. A four-wheel drive came onto the wrong side of the road and hit us head-on. Yes, the car was written off.' Inevitably, they said something like, 'That sounds awful. I hope everyone was all right?'

I didn't know what to say to that, so would usually just say, 'Mostly,' in a tone that (I hope) firmly communicated 'Do not ask me any more about this'. If they did ask more, I blathered on a bit about broken knees, ribs, spleens, liver, etc etc. That made them uncomfortable enough.

I didn't say, 'No, we are not all right. My baby daughter died.' I wanted to be correct and accurate and honest, and I wanted our loss acknowledged, but I had to make a number of these phone calls, get a number of quotes. My composure was stretched thinly enough already. I had functions I needed to perform before disintegrating into a weepy pulp. I couldn't go there; not for a flipping insurance quote, not with someone who would only know me as a voice from a call-centre shift. I couldn't risk the random responses the truth might evoke.

It felt ridiculous, shopping around for insurance when something like this had happened. Everything felt ridiculous, flippant. To continue to live and breathe was a mean joke. I didn't realise I could become so bitter. I didn't really know the meaning of it. But bitter and interesting I could handle, maybe; bitter and boring—trapped in this repetitive, ongoing grief—was much harder.

Even with our new car in the driveway, I hadn't yet brought myself to drive again, let alone lay my hands on a steering wheel. A week later, my brother came to visit, and I asked if he wanted to see our new car. We got in, and he shifted the passenger seat back to make room for his long legs and reclined the seat. I laughed. When he was still living at home, you could always tell when Jeremy had borrowed my dad's car by the ultra-relaxed seat. I got into the driver's seat so I could turn on the stereo and show him the GPS, and, somehow, just like that, I drove him around the block.

•

In the heady, queasy days after that positive pregnancy test in June 2009, I'd started a blog, calling it 'Sesame seed sized dreams'. Rima and I had lain in bed and looked up images of a five-week embryo. At that stage, it was just three layers of cells forming into a neural tube and, all up, approximately the size of a sesame seed. I liked the tangential connection with Lebanese food. *Tahini* (sesame seed paste) is a basic ingredient of many dishes, and sesame seeds appear whole in many other recipes, particularly in *zaatar*, a mix used on the pizza-like *manoushe*, which was one of our favourite weekend breakfasts. I knew that we still faced about a 25 per cent miscarriage rate, so I wasn't about to start building big dreams on this tiny wisp of life within me. Or maybe I was, but I wanted to hedge my bets.

The blog documented the slightly nervous, ridiculous and exciting aspects of being pregnant: having a sizeable bust for the first time in my life, and having to find maternity bras to contain it; strange pregnancy dreams; the frankly bizarre, but wonderful, sensation of feeling someone else's hiccups within your belly. The blog also enabled me to connect with other 'rainbow' families—mainly, lesbian mums—across Australia, the US and UK. Those of us at a similar stage of pregnancy gravitated to one another, wanting to hear how others were faring with the discomforts, dilemmas and delights of building a new human being within your entrails. Knowing that each week of pregnancy was moving us closer, not just to the birth, but also to our move interstate, I was also delighted to discover online a thriving community of Melbourne rainbow families, some of whom would become long-term friends online and in real life.

When I put up my 'what happened' post telling the awful news of our accident, my demographic shifted within days. My post had been linked to on 'Lost and Found Connections Abound', a blog aggregator for those experiencing infertility and pregnancy loss. Some of my regular commenters on the blog left their shocked condolences, never to be heard from again. I was sad but I sympathised. If I had been the one who was still pregnant, I would probably have felt awkward and unsure of what to say. Others moved closer, hearing, empathising, and sharing their own experiences of grief. Of those local to Melbourne, a few offered practical support, creating a depth of friendship that I am still grateful for, nearly eight years on. And in my new demographic, I found a whole 'baby lost' community struggling to make sense of babies dying, and of their own role as bereaved parents.

I sought out their stories. I wanted to know how other people survived this, what was 'normal'. What were you supposed to do when the catastrophic thing—glanced at in all the pregnancy books but never discussed—happened? And what did you do with your days when you'd been all lined up to shush, and wipe bottoms, and barely have a moment to yourself? Conversations with friends and family were mostly about our progress—the girls at school, me getting ready to return to work, settling into our new home and suburb. 'We're getting there,' was my refrain. But where exactly was that? And how could I navigate 'there'?

I was diligent in my grief. I sought out my own homework and devoured it. I hunted out baby lost blogs. I wanted a manual. I wanted practice guidelines, some kind of rules to follow. Anything that would tell me there was a solution.

I wanted to hear other women's stories, but with those stories came all their pain and trauma. Rima would find me at the laptop, tears falling onto the keys. '*Habib*, don't,' she would say. 'You've got enough sadness of your own.' Indeed, there were points when I had to stop reading, turn away, distract myself with TV or Facebook instead. I could feel something shattering in me. This massive ocean of grief—mine and everyone else's—was cracking open the small bathtub I'd allowed for sadness in my life and was leaking out in an unstoppable flood. I had thought that the sad, hard bits of life could be contained—that was what optimism and psychiatric hospitals were for.

I would click away, thinking, 'This stuff will drown me.' How could I hang onto my basic beliefs about the world as an essentially fair and good place in the face of all this sadness, injustice and cruelty?

Yet, a small part of me was relieved to know that it wasn't just me being picked on, that loss and grief were catastrophically normal and common. Somehow, though, I clung onto the idea that there was some maximum amount of pain any one person could suffer. The bathtub was gone, but I thought a full-length, above-ground plastic pool might do the trick.

Baby Lost

Sunday, 21 March 2010

We're getting close to three months since the accident, and it suddenly occurred to me that maybe I wanted to write a three-month letter to Z. I'm not having a dig at those who write letters to their living children—god knows if she'd lived I would have been right on the bandwagon. It is a beautiful idea, that's why I just wanted a little taste of it, even though it isn't quite the same when your baby isn't here to record all the new amazing things they learned and you learned about them each month. But this is part of my task here, to accept that I don't get any more time here on earth with her. It could go like this:

> My darling girl,
> I'm trying to work out how big you might be, if this was your three month birthday rather than three months since you died. We saw a baby today on our way back from the market, probably a bit more on the newborn side than you would be by now. You'll be happy to know that I still haven't seen any baby that comes near you in the looks department, and we seem to be surrounded by them at the moment. They're lovely, they're sweet, but they're not you.
>
> I'm hoping that wherever you are, in the non-denominational, vaguely agnostic Good Place where I like to think you might be 'living the dream', you are growing and learning. Those little legs would be filling out, and maybe you are giving your godparents some smiles, starting to focus on their faces and grin gummily at them. God, I wish we were there to see you and hold you, my love. I wish I could be feeding you and feeling some pride and amazement in your increasing fatness. Rima would be making faces at you, doing her expert babymama thing, teaching you Arabic.
>
> But enough about your milestones, let's talk about mine! I can now bend my knee well over 100 degrees. Woo hoo. And my quadricep muscle now responds when I want to move it. I can get in and out of bed without doing that weird robot-leg move I had

to do before. We're going for big walks, to and from the shops, around the park, with only one crutch—and I won't need that for much longer. We're sleeping through the night a lot more than last month. I think I'll be starting my new job next month—beginning part-time and working my way up to full-time by July.

Your sisters miss you. They are making friends at their new school, and they've freaked them out showing them photos of our wrecked car. They were all geared up to be the best babysitters ever, I hope you know that.

I won't write you a letter every month, I hope you'll understand. But I love you and think about you every day.

With all my love, Mama

16

Scar tissue

In late February 2010 I had my review appointment with the trauma unit at Royal Melbourne. The doctor who saw me introduced himself as Ganesh, and I immediately thought of images of the elephant-headed god. He talked me gently through the CT scans that had been taken on the night of the accident. There was Z, curled in my womb, her hand up near her face. *Oh, my little one.* There was no need for any further scans. The liver and spleen damage seemed to be healing up well, and I wouldn't need to come back.

At home, I made a sketch of my trauma doctor. Like his namesake deity, he had the head and sad, serious eyes of an elephant, but a human body with two arms: one gesturing towards a CT scan, another holding aloft tweezers gripping a bloodied shard of windscreen glass.

I had dreams of walking with my one crutch and a heavy backpack, up hills, through endless train stations, around in circles. Somewhere along the way, I realised I'd left the crutch behind and I'd been walking without it—but, instead of being pleased, I was devastated. I woke and walked stiffly to the bathroom, realising how fond I was of this limp and my crutch as visible signals that I was still wounded. I understood now why people wore black for mourning. It is simpler and less confronting than having to continually convey the message, *'Someone I love has died. I feel irretrievably broken—please go gently with me.'*

Since the accident, I hadn't been able to lift my left leg from the knee. I would sit there, cajoling my foot to rise, but the best it could do was slide forward. The message to lift seemed to fizzle out somewhere between brain and leg. My physio had brusquely assured me this movement would come back, and had focused on breaking down the scar tissue so that I could bend my knee. One day my stepmum, Debbie, a retired physiotherapist, sat down with me.

'You still can't lift this leg?'

'Nope; I can't even remember what it feels like to lift it.'

She patted the couch, saying, 'Both legs up here,' and rolled a towel to prop under my left knee. With a tea towel, she made a little sling for my ankle, so that she could lift my foot.

'Okay. I'm going to help you lift it—but you lift too.'

She lifted it slowly, giving me time to respond. *Move*, I told my leg. And, suddenly, my breath caught with a small sob of pain. When I slowed things down, I realised that my brain wasn't just issuing an unheard 'Move' command—it was also receiving a pain message. I had to receive and listen to the pain message before my leg could override it and lift through the pain. Once I did that, and allowed myself to feel the pain, my foot started lifting out of Debbie's hand.

'Yes; see, you're doing it now!'

It was tiny, but it was movement.

I tried again the next morning, on my own, getting bolder and lifting my whole leg forwards from the knee. It took a few tries, but suddenly my leg was lifting, and I was sobbing—at first with pain, but then from relief, sadness and the effort of it, that such a simple thing could be so hard. In waking up those nerves and calling them into action, I also had to tell them the bad news, and, in doing so, hear their shock and pain from the impact. Even my knee missed her.

Friday, 26 March 2010

I'm dreaming again. I'm in a bathroom like the Sydney Law School one—a long grey infinity of tiles with door after door after door. Margaret Atwood is here—eyes wry, her tight curls moving with her gaze. She is advising me right here in the ladies toilets.

'If you want it, you'll have to get up and do it every day. Even on the days you don't want it. And be honest.' She gives me a sharp look and I open my mouth to say something.

'No, not pretending to be honest—actually being honest.'

I feel like she is stripping the husk off me, roughly, but as though there was something there worth un-husking.

Again, she reads my face, and speaks to me through the mirror this time.

'Yes, indeed—but don't expect me or anyone else to find it ...', she points at me with a slender writing-calloused finger, '... that's your job.'

And she pats my hand. Not in a nanna-like way but briskly, reassuringly.

'You'll get there,' she quotes my own words back at me, 'wherever that is.' She smiles with half-lidded eyes.

'Oh, I know. I'm no writer-goddess. But I am older, and that still counts for something.'

I don't know how to address her. 'Margaret' could refer to all kinds of women of her age.

'Of her age,' I hear her tutting under her breath, still in camera with my thoughts.

'Ms Atwood' isn't specific enough either. I sense that people who know her call her something else, but I wouldn't fall into that category of familiars. Peg? Marg? Her eyebrows ratchet higher with each suggestion. And then she looks at her watch, 'Well, kiddo,' and here I get the first genuine smile—a glow that rolls out across the space between us and warms me. 'Enough fairy godmother time. You take care and don't be a scaredy cat.'

'Yes, ma'am!' I hadn't quite planned to say that, but the words click into place and she smirks an approving smirk.

'See? You'll be fine.'

•

With the girls back at school, Rima and I knocked around the house, untethered by work and with a diminishing number of medical appointments. One weekday, we drove down to Somers and found our way to Z's spot. The ground was still disturbed. It wasn't that long ago we had knelt here, and tapped the plastic bottom of the container to see if any more ashes would fall out. We stood there—unsure of what to do.

I'd never done the grave-visiting thing before. We'd wandered through graveyards out of curiosity, boredom, but never to visit anyone. My grandparents' ashes were somewhere here too, but that grief had been a much neater and more timely affair than the ache to hold our child, to be near her. When we'd chosen this place, I'd thought about the trees, the smell of the beach, the sandy dirt imprinted with our childhood footprints; not about a little hole in the ground. Rima hunted around and found a small chunk of stone to mark the spot. I wanted desperately to fall on the ground, to lay my cheek on the sandy soil, but I was still self-conscious about this grief. We hugged, wept, and, as we left, I patted the strong, curved bough of the gum tree bordering the chapel. *Take care of our gorgeous girl.*

•

Several times a week, I went to the hydrotherapy pool to do the exercises the physio had prescribed. The water was warmer than bath temperature, and I was usually the youngest one in the pool by at least three decades. There was something very comforting about being around the elderly and injured. Stripping down to bathers and exposing my scars was easier around others who were similarly lumpy, limpy and scarred. We had been marked by life in more extreme ways than those in the 'normal' pool. Where once we had wounds, now we had scar tissue telling the history of those wounds, and their healing. Mine were no longer raw cut edges, but new, reddish skin—difficult to stretch and unrecognisable as normal skin. Over time, the redness would fade, but the seams remain; reminders of being broken and being mended. In the hydrotherapy pool, no one really looked one another in the eye, or wondered about the repetitive motions and odd contortions we had to perform, or the adult bath toys we needed to perform them. At the same time, I felt a little like a fraud because my disabilities were (I hoped) temporary. Sometime soon, I could turn my back on the hydro pool—at least until age or injury sent me back.

One day I turned up, and an arthritis aquatherapy class was on in the hydro pool. Reluctantly, I walked back to the lap pool and started doing my exercises in the shallow end. I wasn't the only refugee from the hydro pool—two older Italian women were marching up and down, talking quietly. I was doing okay, even when a heavily pregnant woman started swimming in the next lane. But when she turned and started doing backstroke, her belly submerging and emerging with each stroke, I had to dive deep and close my eyes.

•

At the Preston Market I went to pay for our fruit and vegies. The woman at the cash register turned. There, under her apron, was her broadly pregnant belly. She reciprocated my look at her belly and looked at mine, asking, 'Are you pregnant?'

My tongue rolled back in my head. 'No.' I wanted to say more but the words could not fit out of my mouth and, instead, I stared down at the net bag she had just put my tomatoes in, willing myself through the fine holes.

'Well, have a nice day,' she said.

•

My mum has a thing for new babies. There's a photo of her at a cousin's Christmas party; the usual gathering of my dad's extended family. It's not a posed photo—it captures various conversations between cousins, the slight awkwardness of the biannual catch-up. And there, tucked in the middle, is my mother, holding my cousin's baby son, not quite a week old, locking eyes with him as though no one else existed. A big, raw chunk of intimacy in the midst of the public family–Christmas business.

You hold a baby differently once you've lost one of your own. For my mother, like me, it was her firstborn, a baby girl. Lost, not to stillbirth but to adoption in an era of choicelessness—no reliable information about conception (or contraception); no access to abortion; a family who kicked her out, a boyfriend who didn't want to know, and social workers who told her the best thing she could do for her child was to permanently remove herself from its life. It is hard to coax my mum to talk about what happened. I know she stayed with a friend in Melbourne, and looked after her friend's kids in return for board and lodging. When labour began, she walked to the Women's.

Things often get shaky in November for my mum. November is the season for quiet concern. For the squeak of vinyl armchairs in the TV room of the mental health unit. A birthday that goes unmarked, that floats unspecified over the entire month. Conversations that peter out, questions left hanging while we divert to other, more concrete topics.

So much of my mother disappeared into the dark spaces of her unspeakable grief, windows papered over with layers of shame, of silence; not just hers, but that of family members, and the ones who shamed her. I know there are whole rooms there, filled with specific things. We hear noises from in there. Pipes that rumble, appliances that fizzle in the dark, unknowable, inscrutable. I have given up asking. But I knew that for me, the windows had to be wide open on my grief. This was a loss that anyone who loved me had to know, and know well. Nothing matched, for me, the horror of the locked room, the claustrophobia of a sealed-up grief.

Monday, 3 May 2010

We're sick of the house, sick of our own misery and sick of each other's company. So what is the best remedy for this malcontent? Clearly, wandering around Ikea with legions of pregnant women and parents holding small children lurking behind every Billy bookcase is a fabulous idea.

Things started badly this morning when I woke early, and read the last few chapters of *Northern Lights*. Nothing like young adult sci-fi for comfort reading, or so I'd thought. The book had begun with the irresistibly heartening premise that all humans have their own spiritually-connected talking animal companion—leading me to imagine that I could expect a happy ending, or at the very least a Harry Potter-esque happy-and-safe-for-now ending. But no. Apparently author Philip Pullman has other ideas, which don't include rounding off my escapist bout of children's sci-fi in a gentle enough way so that I can start my Sunday morning without feeling like Armageddon is around the corner.

We entered the Ikea play-house with two very simple objectives, and neither of them was to be reminded that even if we buy all this stuff, our house will never look like an Ikea showroom. I think it must be a genetic thing—either you have the tidy-decluttering-clean-lines-matching-furniture-Ikea gene or you don't, and Rima and I clearly don't. We're not complete grots—we do Make An Effort, and temporarily fight back the jungle on a regular basis—but with three pets and two teenagers, as well as our own messy selves, there is quite a bit of jungle to deal with.

If you've been to one of those water theme parks which has a canal section where everyone floats around the same circular route on giant inflatable donuts, then you may as well have been at Ikea with us, floating along a twisting series of Ikea-ised rooms, bumping up against pregnant tummies and living babies at every turn. I'm not mortally offended by all this evidence of everyone else's fecundity, but it is hard to concentrate on finding soft furnishings while I'm constantly playing games of 'Would she have been about that big by now? Or fatter?'

Eventually, the current brought us along to the cashiers, and we piled our small pieces of pleasantly-smelling wood and Nordic-looking fabric into our tiny reusable carry bags. By then, shopping centre fatigue had set in, and it only took one song to make me weep in the car. From there it was only a short hysterical step to melt-down-land when I got home and realised that there was no tofu in the fridge for the one meal I could imagine making—green Thai curry. It is a sad thing when you feel like you are useless at everything, including feeding your stubbornly vegetarian self some kind of protein on a regular basis.

Somehow, the lack of tofu, and consequent nutritional failure, was the last straw on top of the giant haystack of things I'm not managing to do very well lately, including finding decent work clothes to wear, cleaning the house, being an academic and being a likeable stepmother. It is the state I've come to call Everything is Broken. *But, you've just lost your child, only four months ago—give yourself a break*, as a beloved friend was telling me this morning. Yes, yes. Four months. How long will it take before I can function normally? I was doing it okay two days ago, or at least creating the appearance of it. If things fall apart only every second day, is that progress?

Rima was lovely—Ikea and shopping centres don't seem to have quite the same enervating effect on her. She let me weep all over her in the kitchen, and suggested we order in pizza. Instead, I marched off damp-eyed into the dark to hunt and gather tofu from the supermarket just to prove to myself that I could do the adult thing and make dinner.

•

During my time in hospital and rehab, Mum had been solid—visiting every day, ferrying Rima and the girls around, procuring exactly what was needed before we knew we needed it. We had asked her to stay with us in Preston and help once I'd been discharged, but things were harder than we could have imagined. Mum was sleeping in her campervan in our driveway, but mainly living in the house with us, along with her exuberant red heeler puppy. Sharing the same space and relying on Mum to drive us around and help with the house put new pressures on our relationships. Nothing was right and nothing would be right for some time.

As our situation eased from sharpened emergency to the duller, slower stuff of grief, I could see Mum growing quieter. We wanted help but we also needed privacy. The vague plan had been for her to stay in Melbourne after Haloumi's birth and to enjoy being an *oma*, but now it wasn't clear what she would do. Mum had never been one for winter— the cold and the darkness triggered her depression, turned her inwards towards that dark, sad room. When my brother and sister-in-law told us they wanted to head up to Cairns to train as diving instructors, Mum suggested driving them there in her campervan. And so, she was off, fleeing the advancing Melbourne autumn.

17

Funeral appreciation

Two days after my birthday, I was at work in the law school. I was eating lunch at my desk, a bad habit, and flicked onto Facebook. There was a post from my friend Karin.

She was living in Paris, with her partner, Ned, and their baby, Albert, who had been born in mid-December 2009. We had seen the first photos of him on Christmas Eve at my dad's house, resting the laptop on my huge Z-filled belly, and cooing at his creased feet and dark, thoughtful eyes. They were planning a visit home to Australia in July, and we had plotted a meeting of the babies—hers, mine and Renee's. After the accident I had been so heartbroken that Z would never meet Albert, that they would never be playmates. Karin and Ned were devastated for us. Among their busy-ness with their baby and Paris, Karin stayed in contact, remembered my birthday. But her post on 17 June was brief:

> We lost Albert yesterday. they say SIDS—La mort subite—we cant breath. sorry for telling you this way.

News like this has a rushing sound, like a vandal, like a destructive wind. At first I didn't understand and had to read it again. I wept and called Rima, sent this awful news in her direction. I wept for Karin, for Ned, for little Albert, for us and for Z. I wept because I knew the words to say, because it was all too familiar. I wept for the thought of him growing cold, and for the little voice that said, *It is not just us now.*

In the days and nights that followed, Karin's words pulsed through my head, tapped out like a telegram, over and over again. *La mort subite.* And with it, the thoughts of his little form, lying cold somewhere in a Paris hospital. How could we undo this? What is it about death, that it has to be so damn permanent and non-negotiable? There is no 'maybe' left, only 'never'. I was unable to work, to write, I frittered away time on the blogs, and the baby lost forums, weeping for all these babies. And on a friend's blog, I came across the concept of tonglen meditation:

> When things are painful and difficult, the quality of difficulty should remind us to have the thought, 'Other people feel this.' Isolation in our pain and the loneliness of our burden reminds us of our shared humanity.

I'd found solace in meditation before; in the short meditations within yoga classes, and in a meditation group at Newcastle University. Often in yoga, the instruction was to breathe in light or energy, and to breathe out anything you didn't need; a pranic version of the tiny transfers of oxygen and carbon dioxide our lungs performed with every breath. Tonglen meditation ran counter to this logic. It instructs you instead to breathe in the hot, dark, heavy feelings of sadness, anger, of feeling stuck—not just for you but anyone else feeling the same way—and then to breathe out a sense of spaciousness, of light, of safety, of relief from suffering. There was a generosity to it that went beyond our own biologically acquisitive nature of bringing nutrients in, sending waste out. In biological terms, this was photosynthesis; taking in the unwanted carbon dioxide, sending out the oxygen that was needed—and in the process generating something new, an unexpected sweetness.

Funeral appreciation

With tonglen I could breathe in those hammering words and the dark, sickly fever of *la mort subite*—for us, and for Karin, Ned and Albert. I could let the sadness shake me and be absorbed into my cells. And I could breathe out relief from the hammering, and the wish for his little spirit to be somewhere warm, somewhere good. And that he might just bump into Z and make knowing baby eyes at her. 'You too, huh?'

My birthday present to myself was a t-shirt printed with a graphic of an African elephant in full charge. Dokkoon, the Indian elephant at Melbourne Zoo, had safely delivered her baby in February, but in following her progress I'd also discovered that zoo elephants have much higher infant mortality than do wild or semi-captive populations. I felt a solidarity for the elephant mothers left behind. Wearing my elephant t-shirt enabled me to get out of bed, to make decisions without tears, to feel maybe I could be like a mama elephant—all the more fierce with love because of my loss.

We flew to Sydney for Albert's funeral. After the ceremony in the chapel, we followed Karin and Ned, carrying their boy to his grave. The Port Botany wind blew up the cliffs to meet us. It was a big crowd for a small person. On the way back up the hill, I saw Renee. We hugged, this time shaking with sobs, no big bellies between us. My brain knew that I couldn't turn this into a statistic—that it is not normal, or usual, for two out of three babies to die. Certainly not in countries with modern medical care, certainly not for women educated to postgraduate level. Later, Karin and I stood looking at Renee's baby, Anna, and held onto one another. 'She'll be our measuring-stick baby,' said Karin. 'That's how big our babies would be. She will always be the right age.'

Sunday, 11 July 2010

> It's been a season of grief. Our own grief is becoming worn and supple, though it still catches at our heels, constrains the way we walk. We limp as veteran mourners into the new fresh grief of Karin and Ned for their tiny son, not quite six months old, and my cousin

for her husband of 22 years. I'd never been to a funeral of someone younger than 60 before (how fortunate! what lucky planet was I living on?)—but we've been to two within a week now, and three in the last seven months if you count our baby daughter's.

I now have a new appreciation for funerals—the time that goes into them, the importance of the small details, the careful, deliberate laying-down of ritual and memory. We sit on hard wooden benches, search for tissues, give much longer than usual hugs.

How precious it is to have a festival for the lost one you treasured—to put them in the centre, include them in the party one last time. At the funeral, two incompatible realities collide: 'He is gone forever, we must say goodbye' and 'He will always be here with us, in our hearts'. Nothing can stitch those two opposites into a cohesive story, but this is the heaving, fractal reality. Instead we have to re-stitch our hearts around it—or let them break, brittle, on the floor. It hurts to stitch our hearts like this, when the needle goes in we think we cannot bear it a moment longer. We think everything our hearts are made of will shatter. Yet the laws of physics bend once again, and so do our hearts—sore and tortured by the thread, pulled painfully back into something heart-shaped.

I wished so much I could offer some sage advice to Karin and Ned on how to survive this loss, but the truth is that I'm no closer to finding 'the secret' than they are. Surely, it isn't helpful to say, 'If your loss is anything like ours, you will struggle to stay sane and find meaning, you will feel broken for a long time and your loss will creep its way into everything—your work, your sex life, your friendships, and into the minutiae of what you wear and how you cook.'

It's the truth—but it is also true that we have times when things feel good, when it feels like the edges are coming together and we can laugh. And even if we did know the secret (I'm still hopeful) it would nonetheless be our secret to our loss, and would likely be helpless in the lock of their sadness.

Funeral appreciation

I was so hesitant about coming back to Sydney—to look at these 'before' places where the imprint of being pregnant and pre-accident is so fresh. But once we were here, things were nowhere near as raw as I had imagined. Yes, I was here before—we drove these streets in our now-dead car, my tummy rounded and living, full of our now-dead baby. But things were wound-back then, and it felt surprisingly good to remember that witless hopefulness and presumption that everything would be okay. We drove past our old house and parked across the road, and I thought of the last time we pulled the front door shut behind us.

We were sweaty and gritted with the dust that emerged from behind the furniture. It had been humid since I'd woken up in the summer morning dark, to keep filling boxes. From eight weeks of pregnancy, Haloumi had been waking me early, but that morning it was my excitement as well as hers that propelled me out of bed—this was the day, the day we moved. What kind of insanity was this—to be moving an entire family interstate while I was nearly eight months pregnant? My own insane optimism, and the broad-braided rope of homesickness, were pulling me back to Melbourne. After so many hours, our hands papered with corrugated cardboard and the sweetness of packing tape on our teeth, the truck had finally left. Inside it, our things were packed tight like tetris blocks—an entire family life condensed into so many square metres. We'd tiptoed across the damp-mopped floors with the real estate agent to sign off on the condition report. The electricity company man had come and read the meter, and switched off the power. We'd wiped the place clean of our existence there.

The car was loaded with all our holiday things—I took it to fill up on petrol while Rima and the girls walked to the chicken shop, then parked it across the road, its nose pointing west to the M5, and Melbourne beyond that. We couldn't go back into the house—we'd just handed the keys in. So we sat there eating takeaway chicken and chips on the nature strip across the road from our house (no longer our house) having an impromptu picnic—relishing for a moment all the work of packing and the relief of finishing it.

    I had worked so hard—to convince Rima to make the move at all, to get the job leading us back, to organise the move, and in the last weeks, to sift and pack our things while finishing up at work and dashing to pre-natal yoga. At times my mum or Rima or the removalists had told me to sit down and have a break, but I felt strengthened by my very-pregnant state, not weakened by it. My belly was heavy, but even in my sweaty dirty state, sitting on the nature strip eating takeaway, I felt like a trailer-trash goddess—beautiful and potent.

    Not that potent, as it turned out. But sitting in the car nearly seven months later with a saggy belly and our baby girl reduced to ashes, I could still feel the humidity of that December afternoon on the grass and remember my optimism.

18
I have a dark-haired daughter

I started my new job not as the promising recruit, but grief-shattered and limping. I had a 'return to work' coordinator, who asked me about my physical limitations and fatigue levels but didn't canvas how to interact professionally when you felt like a walking piece of roadkill.

Ours was a quiet corridor, doors mostly shut. I took to wandering the campus at lunchtime, and soon found a garden enclosed by a quadrangle, lush with wide-leafed cherry trees, where there was a memorial stone for a woman who'd died in 2008, Kathleen. Here at least was someone I had something in common with, I joked with myself darkly. But still, I often joined Kathleen for lunch, and discovered that if you sat still long enough, her other friends appeared. There were tiny, spherical blue wrens and sometimes other birds—magpies, of course, and clear-eyed ravens, and sometimes a New Holland honeyeater, with a streak of yellow on its brow. I still couldn't quite convince myself of the idea that Z was somewhere else, but I found the birds a comfort. *Tell her I love her*, I would tell them, *if you happen to see her*. I had always dismissed birdwatching as the daggiest of hobbies, but now I found myself looking up bird identification websites, and calling my dad to describe a new sighting.

I cried the first time I saw a pair of red-rumped grass parrots, and was immediately mortified. Part of it was the shock. They were so well camouflaged that when my eyes focused and I realised what I was seeing, it was as though they had appeared out of nowhere. But with that was a miraculous sense of coming home to beauty, right under my nose. As though Z were saying, *What? I've been here all along.*

•

At the end of November 2009, I was giving my last lectures and seminars before starting my maternity leave, waddling around the university and feeling enormously, deliciously pregnant. In among the rush of teaching and busy preparations at home for the move to Melbourne, I dashed off an abstract for a conference in Singapore in July 2010. Haloumi would be nearly six months old, surely old enough for us to have gotten the hang of baby-wrangling, and for me to have enough brain space to present a conference paper. The future with a baby in it was impossible to imagine; making plans for 2010 felt like being blindfolded and sticking a pin in a map. But it sounded like a great conference, and I loved the idea of travelling overseas with our baby.

It was March 2010 when I got the email letting me know my paper had been accepted. It was like a letter from outer space that took light years to arrive—the Hannah who had written that abstract was long dead. And yet here I was, answering to the same name, but the future we had expected had never arrived; instead I was stuck in this alternate reality of being a babyless mother. At first I dismissed it. I couldn't even summon the energy to reply, or to decide how much of our sad tale to tell the organisers when declining the invitation. But as autumn set in, and I gritted my teeth and started my new job, the thought of a trip to Singapore in the midst of a Melbourne winter looked more appealing. It wasn't too late to apply, and maybe it could be a good thing for Rima and me to have a break, and for me to get my research moving again.

I couldn't get funding for the trip, but I needed a date to work towards, so I accepted and started making travel plans.

As June and July dissolved into more grief and sadness, I thought, 'I've made a terrible mistake—I won't be able to do this. The bit of me that could draw research together and write is gone.' I'd forgotten how much work it was to write up a conference paper, and as the departure date approached, I felt more and more panicked. But I had to come up with something.

And, somehow, I did. It was only after I became too tired to be tired, and too panicked by the deadline to panic, that from weariness came something that was there all along. For a little while, I had my concentration back, and I could look at all my work and pull the threads together, say what I needed to say. It was such a relief, to get a taste of that pre-accident me, to remember that I was still there, that the sadness hadn't wiped away everything.

When we arrived in Singapore, we stripped away the layers of Melbourne winter clothes we had worn on the plane. Each layer of clothing seemed to wind us back in time, towards summer and the black hole that was 27 December 2009. Early the next morning, while Rima was still sleeping in, I snuck out of our room and made my way to the pool on the hotel rooftop. I wore the same one-piece bathers that my sister had lent me for my hydrotherapy sessions to strengthen my knee; they'd become saggy with all the chlorine at the local indoor pool. I was nervous relinquishing my towel and walking to the pool—my body still felt like hospital property, all staple marks and scars and wasted muscle. But the water greeted me with its familiar silkiness and I discovered I could still comfort myself with slow, deliberate movement. I closed my eyes and summoned back the feeling of swimming with Haloumi swimming in my belly—a buoyant equilibrium between inside and outside. 'I have a dark-haired daughter.' My hands pushed through the water. She can't be erased. 'I have a dark-haired daughter.'

•

At the conference, it felt odd to be mingling with people in my professional capacity again, rather than as a patient or as a shy colleague. In every conversation, there was a little wall I needed to step over as I decided whether or not to disclose that, just seven months ago, I had held my dead child in my arms. I had worried that when it was time to give my paper, my voice would fail me, that it might betray my brokenness. But in the immediacy of the conference, and my desire to do justice to my research and the paper I had prepared, I felt less broken than I had in months.

After the conference, we took a bus and then a boat out to a tiny Malaysian island. We were adrift not only in the South China Sea, but when nighttime came, in the middle of the Milky Way. I've never seen so many stars.

One of the lovely things friends did for us after Z died was to band together and name a star after her. They gave us a chart, a certificate and the coordinates. After a few unsuccessful attempts at finding her particular star, with zero astronomical knowledge (and without a telescope), we took to appropriating whichever star we liked as 'her' star. Usually, for me, it was the first star I would see in the west as I was walking home from the tram after work. But that night on the island, our heads together and our toes in the sand, Rima and I saw a shooting star, and it felt as if she'd sent it for us—a tiny, solitary Haloumi firework.

19

Dr No-Sperm-for-You

After I got out of hospital, after the memorial service, after all the physio appointments, after I had started my transition back to work, after all the news and drama had settled down—I hit a wall. I had been so focused on 'getting there'; coping, dealing with the basic survival tasks in front of me. I had imagined that this grief was something to be got through—a swamp, if not a mountain to be got over. I didn't expect a great big wall of 'my baby died' staring me in the face every morning.

Worse, what I had thought was the whole wall was only one particular bit of it, because I'd been standing so close. I took a step back and blinked, and there was the wall; higher and wider than I could see, with no edge in sight in any direction. 'Right. Wall. Wall as far as the eye can see. Shit.' I thought of cartoons of people imprisoned for life, carving lines in the wall to mark the years, finishing with a skeleton leaning back against it.

Now that I could amble up the road to the library by myself, I decided this was my project. Surely others had scaled this wall before, or found a loose brick, a secret door. I would research my way right over this wall and away from it. 'Stillbirth', I typed into the catalogue. 'Neonatal death'. 'Grief'. I ordered books from neighbouring libraries,

I waited for parcels of books ordered online. *Tell me your secret*, I whispered desperately into their dust jackets, *how do I fix this?* I had started researching and reading with the thought that I would find an answer, that I would 'get religion', or hear the secret from mothers who had somehow been 'healed' after their child's death. This was what kept me going: the thought that there was a way through, that there was an answer to all my sadness out there somewhere—a key, a secret formula. I worked on it like it was a maths problem. I followed each line of reasoning carefully, and tried not to cry when they all led back to another spot with a good view of the wall.

I found three main answers. The first was boring old Time. Fat use that was. I needed to fix this pain right now! What was I supposed to do—put myself into a deep freeze until the requisite amount of time passed and I could wake up feeling human again? 'Time' did not involve me doing anything; it was beyond my control. The second answer I didn't like either, because it suggested that, actually, this grief wasn't fixable. Rather, it was me who would have to adapt to it and learn to live with it in time—taking me back to my objections to answer number one.

The third wasn't exactly presented as 'the answer', but I surmised it from the fact that every book or story I read about perinatal death featured a subsequent child. Here was a nice, practical solution: have another baby. And while I couldn't guarantee results, this was the only option I felt I could actually do anything about. I knew, of course, that one baby couldn't replace another, that Z would always have a special place in our hearts, but I wanted a child I could parent, in the earthly, messy way of living children. I was impatient with the slow repetition of my grief. I needed a sweetener, a happy ending, resolution of the narrative. I stopped writing and went into waiting mode—waiting for a happy ending on which to finish our story.

•

Dr No-Sperm-for-You

I was at the Korean jewellers in a small arcade in Preston, handing over a small ziplock bag containing a fine, but heavy, chain. The woman opened the bag and laid the chain on a velvet board, poking it into a line with one little finger. This was the spot where the ambulance officer's scissors bit, snapping the gold chain between their silver blades. The chain had run like a rivulet into his cupped hand. And, in its place, he negotiated a foam and plastic neckbrace behind my head, and velcroed it into place, careful not to catch my hair.

The chain had been broken for seven months now. I explained what happened, and that I'd like it mended but with a small gold heart to mark the mending spot. 'I was in a car accident—they cut my chain—our baby died.' It was enough for her to get it and she gasped, 'Awww!' and put her hand on mine. 'Awww! We will make you happy!'

•

Happy and mended is what we wanted, and so, after waiting the minimum six or so months recommended by the obstetrician, we were in hot pursuit of the one thing that we imagined could deliver that state: a positive pregnancy test. But before we could have a shot at pregnancy, there was paperwork to fill out, and administrative hoops to leap through—police checks, child welfare record checks, applications to the treatment authority to import the frozen sperm from New South Wales to Victoria, counselling and consents. Many of these hoops we had already jumped when we started the process in Sydney, but because each state had its own fertility treatment laws, we had to repeat our efforts in Melbourne. When we explained our story and Z's loss, the staff apologised but there was nothing they could do.

In the calendar, we'd circled August as the month where we could leap from the grief roller coaster onto the trying-to-conceive roller coaster; or, better still, perform some Evel Knievel feat of riding both roller coasters at once. August was the month that had been pulling me forwards, getting me through. We had diligently submitted all our paperwork; arranged for our donor, Jorge, to fly down from Sydney for repeat counselling; submitted to blood tests both for me and Rima. But when day one of my cycle arrived, and I called the clinic to work out the treatment schedule, I discovered that our euphemistically titled 'samples' had arrived from New South Wales, but without the requisite paperwork and without the requisite tests having been carried out on them. We carefully packed up our hopes and bundled them into the diary for September. By then, the tests would have all been carried out and we'd be able to press ahead with an insemination.

Sunday, 29 August 2010 Inside-out Day

Friday was the 27th—eight months since our accident. I was trying to figure out why it felt so much harder than seven months. We were in Singapore at the seven month mark, and somehow felt like we were 'on holiday' from the grief. I'd just given my conference paper and we had a little holiday ahead of us. I felt close to Z, but the grief felt distant, smoother. Eight months isn't half a year, it didn't make sense for it to be any harder than seven months. The answer was so obvious it took me a while to realise. She lived eight months in my belly, and from now on she would have been dead longer than she existed. I spent eight months gearing up to be a mother, and then the pendulum swung back, and I feared that my whole pregnancy has now unwound—that I'm back to where I started. We've now spent more time grieving her than I was pregnant. Babies that were conceived on the night ours died will be born soon.

    I dreamt last night that someone was giving away a baby car seat and pram for free, and Rima and I were discussing—is it too soon to start buying baby things again? I woke, and she'd had a very similar dream—that we'd won baby things in a competition, and were toying with the idea of bringing them home.

Dr No-Sperm-for-You

Maybe this means we are ready to start again, to push the pendulum back in the direction of hope.

•

September arrived, and with it, dire test results about our frozen sperm samples. The same samples that had given our Sydney fertility doctor cause to wax lyrical about their vitality and motility were, when defrosted, only 7 per cent motile. The freezing process, it seemed, had turned our little Usain Bolts into Grampa Simpsons. I wasn't giving up, though, and continued to call the clinic—even with lousy odds, could we still go ahead with an insemination, if for no other reason than so that I could feel like we were doing something? While the rest of the country was waiting to see whether Julia Gillard would be able to form government after a hung election, I was waiting for a phone call from our clinic.

When the phone call came, we eked out a little more hope. We would be able to go ahead with an insemination, but first we needed to make an appointment with the doctor, so she could explain in person exactly how lousy our chances were. I was happy to leap through another hoop, but when I called to try make the appointment, we found she was booked out for another four weeks.

It felt like torture by bureaucracy. No matter how many people I called or how many times I trotted out our sad saga, I couldn't speak directly with any of the people who could change the decision. I knew there was something a little unhinged about my desperation, yet still I left messages for our doctor, both at her clinic and at her private rooms, furious that the one thing I'd been surviving for over the past eight months could be derailed by something as trivial as appointment availabilities. I was ready for a miracle, any moment now. I thought I could hope it into existence. I was furious with these delays. *Don't you know you are standing between us and our miracle baby!*

Sure enough, an appointment magically opened up, and the next day, Rima and I found ourselves face to face with Dr No-Sperm-for-You.

Yes, she knew how important this was to us, given our recent loss. Yes, there was sufficient sperm. But no, we couldn't have it—not for a clinic insemination (because of the low motility) and not for a take-home insemination (because our donor had not specifically consented to that at the time of the donation, back in 2007). There would be no September cycle. Our consolation prize was a medical certificate. Given our history, she was willing to class me as medically sub-fertile, and therefore eligible for a Medicare rebate on IVF and ICSI treatment—something she would recommend, given the low motility of the thawed sperm. It was as though we'd taken our old Commodore to the mechanics for repairs, only to be told, 'This one won't work again, but we've got a very nice Mercedes we could sell you.' I didn't want a Mercedes, and I certainly didn't want IVF; not if there was still a chance we could conceive via simpler means.

I moped for a while, but sparked up after a message from our donor that he was going to be back in the country in October, and was willing to make a fresh donation for an at-home insem, just as he had back in May 2009. There would be an October cycle, regardless of the pronouncements of Dr NSFU. The hope that we'd stretched back like a rubber slingshot, from August to September to October, could finally be released, catapulting our hopes into movement. *Dear Universe, it happened once. Please let it happen again.* I just wanted that feeling of small knees and elbows tapping out a message, that warmth and potential. I wanted to finish the story this time—not with a memorial service, and condolence cards and a small amount of ashes falling through our hands, but with a new little voice crying, and baby eyes that opened and moved.

By the time we flew home from Sydney after an October weekend of turkey baster-related activities, the broad beans I'd pushed into the dirt in the cool, weepy days of April were towering with flowers and ripening bean pods. We made our first harvest, slipping the bright green beans from their pods and wishing the fecundity might rub off on us too.

Dr No-Sperm-for-You

Tuesday, 26 October 2010

It's day one again, and even though it is the first month we've tried since losing Z, it still feels like Groundhog Day. As philosophical as I can be in my head about percentages and buying our lottery ticket, flipping our coin and whatever stupid metaphor you want to use, I'm still crushed because I'm a dirty hope addict, and I really did think something miraculous might happen.

20
Heartbeat

There was a day when my heart started beating again.

Once I was back at work, Penny and I signed up for a Thursday night beginners yoga class. We'd both done yoga before, but this was a back-to-basics approach—a careful and precise dissection of all the familiar asanas and the movement into and out of them. The teacher was a former dancer; tiny, delicate, but exact and rock-solid. I'd come to know and love the sun salute as my five-minute wake-up routine for the early mornings when I took the 4.30 a.m. train to Newcastle for work, back in the misty land of 'before'. It shook the zombiness of deep sleep from my limbs. I could shower the night before and I could eat breakfast on the train, but without those five minutes of yoga I couldn't gather the wakefulness to put clothes on and get out the door.

But now we took apart each step of the sun salute and pored over the mechanics, cleaned each component, moved and oiled it, and then slowly started reconnecting the pieces. We found the moments within the cycle to inhale into—opening, stretching—and the ones that need an exhalation, pushing with our breath, as well as with our muscles, to exact an alignment, to create momentum, to press our palms into one another or the floor, and release into a deeper stretch. It took us eight weeks of classes to complete the cycle, to return to an upright stance, hands in prayer position, bodies warm from the movement.

'Press each point of your fingers and palms together, like mirror images,' the teacher said. 'Let your thumb bones press into one another and let the knuckles cosy into your breastbone, so you can feel your heart beating.'

I did, and there, against all expectations, was my heart—knocking warmly against my thumbs. Big, hot tears spilled out and scorched down my cheeks.

This is my heart. My big, noisy heart, which kept banging on as Z's small, fast one slowed and then stopped. The enormity of that engulfed me, with anger, that my heart could so callously continue, and thankfulness that it did; that its familiar beat held her and sang to her as hers faded. And there was surprise; that I was, indeed, alive—that, despite the massive impossibility of continuing on without my child, my heart just kept on at its work, wearily, faithfully, persistently.

•

As I re-engaged with my PhD work, in reading my way back into the literature on DNA paternity testing, I came across a mention of a biological phenomenon called maternal-fetal microchimerism—the persistence of fetal DNA within the mother's body for decades after a pregnancy. These were not just fragments, but whole new stem cells. One study found fetal cells replicating within the mothers' bone marrow over fifty years after their children had been born. In mother mice with liver disease, fetal cells were found to 'contribute to the repairing process'.[1] Tears dripped onto my keyboard. Z's cells were right here—pumping through my heart, replicating in my very marrow—and may very well have helped heal the liver and spleen lacerations I had sustained in the crash.

The question that had been dogging me, of where Z went; what if I could answer it literally? Rather than having to decide on a spiritual story for her, in some religion or other, or imagine her in a heavenly elsewhere, what if I could trace the different elements of her—physical and psychological—here in this world? What if she literally still existed in all of those places? As a memory in my brain; as dark and light specks of ash in the sandy soil at Somers; as a fragment of DNA still replicating in my cells; or as small units of energy, unleashed in the heat of her cremation and still bumping their way through the universe? I had half-expected that, in the wilds of my grief, I might find God. What I hadn't imagined was that I could find solace in science.

There was something about the persistence of atoms and energy that I found comforting. Heaven, perhaps, was not a separate elsewhere, but a continuity in elemental form—a photon sparkling on water, or a molecule transforming from dirt to food to living thing and back again.

21
Making the judge cry

Rima and I had made a deliberate decision after the accident not to invest too much in the criminal proceedings against the driver who caused our accident. I'd seen enough in my time as a litigator that I didn't expect a lot in the way of resolution, let alone healing, from the court process. That work lay elsewhere.

All I'd seen in the moments before our accident was the four-wheel drive. Like a drunk at a party, it had bumped up against a sedan travelling alongside it in the next lane, before lurching directly into our path. I'll admit that I wasn't fond of the large, petrol-guzzling vehicles before our accident, but afterwards, that dislike transformed into something else. Just walking past the bulky frame of a four-wheel drive, I could feel my shoulders tensing, my teeth clenching, and the sight of one on the road triggered tears and an open-mouthed horror.

On a windy September day, I armed myself with two of my oldest and dearest friends and attended the Commodore driver's committal hearing. Unusually, the defendant's lawyer wanted to cross-examine several witnesses, including me. We arrived early at the Office of Public Prosecutions building and were seen into a waiting room. The solicitor handling our matter warned us, 'We're not sure if the defendant's solicitor will turn up'; there was some confusion about whether he'd ceased acting. The waiting room had a large, opaque window that faced the street, and blurred figures of people walked past while we sat turning pages of magazines, as if that would make time move faster.

The solicitor returned with a smile. 'Okay, we're on—looks like he's showed up, after all.'

I grabbed awkwardly at my bag and fumbled for my phone, and we were bundled into the hallway. We joined the other solicitors and police officers in that small space, and one of the men put out his hand to me and introduced himself.

I smiled politely; it was a familiar name. 'Oh, hi. You're one of the police officers I spoke to on the phone?'

'No, no. I was driving the Pajero.'

His words moved through my ears and solidified like ice through my bloodstream. In the eight months since the accident, I'd gritted my fear in my teeth in order to get back in a car, to cross a road, and, finally, to drive. But I still couldn't see a four-wheel drive without flinching. I knew intellectually that he wasn't at fault, that he was as much a victim of this accident as I was. My body and some older, more survival-related part of my brain, however, only knew what it had experienced—the sight of several tonnes of Pajero hurtling towards me and my family, and the bone-breaking, placenta-tearing sensation of impact.

'I just wanted to say I'm so sorry.' He leant in for a hug.

I felt myself recoil, and then try to correct it. 'Oh.' *Pause. Gulp. Breathe. Remember that I need to respond.* 'You were hurt too. How are you going?'

'Not so good. I haven't worked since the accident.'

Somehow, we were able to fill the space between us with words again, but he'd felt me recoil. And I'd pulled away from another human being at the very moment he sought my forgiveness.

The cross-examination itself was less charged. The defence barrister was vaguely familiar, but it wasn't the time for figuring out how we knew one another. He quizzed me on the TomTom GPS system I'd given Rima for Christmas, to help her navigate Melbourne, and that we had been using for the first time on the day of the accident. Had I been looking down? How long was I looking at the GPS for? He seemed to fret over my answers. None of this was helping. I had never appeared in this courtroom, but in that formal space felt more like my lawyer self; able to be clear about what I could and couldn't remember, and to tune out the emotional static that usually accompanied talking about 27 December.

It was several weeks later, when Sydney friends were visiting and we'd taken them to a pub, that the prosecutor rang with some surprising news: 'The driver has pled guilty.' The next step was sentencing. The prosecutor got in touch with us and let us know that we could prepare victim impact statements. We could decide whether we wanted to read them ourselves during the sentencing hearing or have the prosecutor read them for us.

Rima decided she didn't want to be there on the day. She didn't want to see the defendant, and wasn't certain how she would react. But if my statement was going to be read out, I wanted to be the person reading it. There was so much in our situation that I had zero control over, so, at the very least, I wanted to tell it in my own words. I wasn't going to enter into the debates about whether our driver should instead have been charged with dangerous driving causing death. What mattered to me was to make our daughter visible, not as a creepy generic 'unborn child' or an object lesson for debates about abortion, but in our relationship with her changeling form: as a long-held hope; as a tiny leap in my belly; as a mysterious, moving bump; and, finally, as a serious-looking but unbreathing baby.

The sentencing hearing was set for early November.

·

Tuesday, 14 September 2010

> I was nearly four years old when Azaria Chamberlain disappeared. The controversy surrounding her mother, Lindy Chamberlain—who

was accused of murdering 9-week-old Azaria—formed such an interwoven part of the cultural carpet of growing up in Australia in the 1980s, that it took me a while to realise, first, what an extraordinary woman Lindy Chamberlain is, and second, that I now have several things in common with her. It bothers me that I have some kind of cultural cringe in saying these two things. But when I read her letter, published in the newspaper to mark thirty years since Azaria's disappearance, it hit me like a tonne of bricks:

> 'It is hard to believe it is thirty years today since my darling baby was taken.
> 'For some odd reason everyone says you will soon forget.
> 'Why is it that people expect me to forget a part of myself? Why would you? Loss of a loved one, particularly a child, is not something you forget any more than you can get out of your mind that you once attended school.
> 'That does not mean you dwell on it all the time. It is simply there in the fabric of your life and history. In some ways it seems forever and in others it is like yesterday still.'

For all the movies and telemovies and tabloid newspapers and magazine coverage, I had somehow forgotten that this woman lost her baby—lost her beloved 9-week-old daughter. And suddenly I thought, here is a woman who has survived babyloss—and she seems so functional. Not just losing a daughter (and never having the chance to say goodbye, because her body was never found), but on top of that, being accused of killing your baby as part of some cult ritual, enduring more trials, inquests and royal commissions than have ever been held on the one issue in Australia, being jailed and separated from her living children for over three years, and being at the centre of a media circus for much of two decades. And yet, here she is, self-possessed and able to articulate her position clearly and passionately. I think she deserves some credit for that.

Making the judge cry

I also think of Lindy whenever I have one of those awkward moments when I'm out somewhere and I've pulled it together and am actually enjoying talking to people, but then I have to tell someone what happened to us, and their natural reaction is shock and sadness. They look at me, and I'm not weeping and falling to pieces, in fact, I want the conversation to move on, and I wonder whether they think I'm some monster who doesn't care that her baby died. I need a little sign that says, 'Yes, I do care. This is the saddest thing that has ever happened to me. My grief is huge and voracious and has eaten huge amounts of my time and energy and personality. But right now, I've got it on a leash and feel like I'm in control of it. Don't start poking at it now, or it will chew my leg off before your very eyes. I need my grief to behave in public, for my own sanity and dignity.'

I wonder—why do I care so much about whether people think I'm grieving 'enough' or in the ways that they would expect? What standard am I trying to perform to here? If I don't fit within one stereotype ('good grieving mother, tragic, weeping') does that automatically push me into another stereotype ('bad, uncaring mother')? And this is where it comes back to Lindy, and back to the way she was demonised by the media for appearing to be 'cold' when she had to give evidence at her trial for her daughter's murder. We grieve in the shadow of all these myths surrounding Lindy Chamberlain. For me it is a reminder of why we need feminism—to remember the force that stereotypes have over women, the way in which our bodies and stories are so often appropriated for other people's purposes. That sometimes we need to claw away all the stereotypes and speak for ourselves.

I have to give evidence tomorrow. Unlike Lindy, I won't be on trial for killing my daughter (someone else will be, though he's charged with dangerous driving causing serious injury, not with murder). But I'll be thinking of Lindy, and wearing sunglasses on the steps of the courthouse in her honour, and in memory of Z and Azaria and all the babies that we wish were here with us.

On the morning of the sentencing hearing, I wore my babushka brooch over my heart, and slipped Z's photo into an envelope placed in the pages of my statement, so that I could touch it while I was reading.

Victim Impact Statement (Nov 2010)
I found it hard to sit down and write this statement, because it is impossible to fit into words the impact of the defendant's dangerous driving and the resulting crash on my life. For a long time I really wondered whether I had died and started a new, different life, because everything was so unrecognizable, including my own body and personality.

Just seeing a car accident on TV grips me with terror and leaves me crying. Big four-wheel drives still frighten me. The sound of ambulances, lying on my back, sitting in a car, putting my right hand to my head—all these things trigger shock and trauma. It is a marathon effort to get dressed, to get to work, to try and bring my mind to a task. The scars on my legs, arm, head and abdomen remind me every day of what it feels like to be crushed by broken metal. But the biggest impact is the least measurable—it is the growing space that our daughter would have had in our lives, had she survived.

Let me tell you about our daughter. She was conceived in Sydney in May 2009 after nine months of unsuccessful fertility treatments, and several years before that of finding a sperm donor and going through counselling processes and quarantine periods as part of the fertility process. We weren't going to tell the girls about the pregnancy until we'd had a scan confirming the pregnancy, but they guessed because we were smiling so much.

At fifteen weeks of pregnancy I first felt her move, like a little goldfish in my belly. We nicknamed her 'Haloumi'. Soon we were getting lots of kicks, and when she stretched, you could see my whole belly move. Her favourite (or, I was hoping, least favourite) music was Rod Stewart—every time he came on the radio she would kick. I was lucky enough to have a healthy, smooth pregnancy. Each night, Jackie and Jasmin would pat my tummy and say 'goodnight Haloumi'.

About a week before the accident we had just moved to Melbourne so that we could be close to my family, and so I could take up a job after my maternity leave finished that wouldn't require so much commuting. The interstate move combined with both Rima and me preparing to go on leave had made it a busy, stressful time, and we were looking forward to spending Christmas with family, and had booked a holiday house for two weeks in January so we could have some quiet family time before the birth.

Four days before the accident, I had an ultrasound and Rima and the girls and my mum and sister came along, and we saw her, very squished up by now, but heart beating strongly and headed in the right direction. At my last midwife visit, the midwife showed me how to feel her back, her legs, her little hand, through my belly. On the morning of the accident, we were at a picnic, and she was hiccuping.

When the four-wheel drive hit our car, and we came to a stop, Rima kept asking, 'Can you feel Haloumi moving?' I didn't answer because I could see what I thought was petrol pouring from the other car and I was scared it would blow up. I told Rima and the girls to get out of the car. I couldn't get out myself—the car was crushed around my legs.

Rima and the girls went to different hospitals, so I was left by myself while the doctors tried and tried to find her heartbeat, and when they finally told me she'd died I had to tell Rima over the phone that our baby hadn't made it. I was induced, and was having six minute long contractions while I was having blood transfusions, while the nurses extracted the glass from my arm, and while my head wound was stapled, re-stapled, and finally stitched because it kept leaving me drenched in blood. Early the next morning, my daughter was born by caesarean section. My dad and mum and sister held her while the surgeons repaired my broken knee. When I came around from the anaesthetic, the first thing I saw was my midwife coming towards me with a photo, saying, 'You had a little girl.'

She was 2500g (5 pound 8) and 48cm long—the length I was when I was born. She had dark curly hair and skin softer than rose petals. She looked calm, but with a slightly worried brow.

I am so sad for Jackie, Jasmin and Mariam who lost their little sister, for my parents, who lost their first grandchild, for my sister and brother, who lost their first niece. Z was so loved and we were all so ready to welcome her.

We have thirty-six photos of our daughter. This is all we will ever get. We have her hand print in black ink, and her footprints. There is a drop of her blood on a blanket we wrapped her in. We didn't take a lock of her hair. I wish we'd known at the time to do that.

What breaks my heart is all the things I can't tell you about my daughter, the things I will never know—the colour of her eyes, the sound of her voice, the things that help her get to sleep, how her sisters make her laugh. So many things we can only ever hypothesise about—would she be crawling by now? What foods would she have reached for? Would she be keeping us up all night? Would she have enjoyed her granddad's singing? Would she be comforted by her Oma's kisses? What kind of little girl might she have been? What kind of young woman?

It seems so strange that all these possibilities—a whole lifetime's worth of them—could have disappeared in one stupid moment on Warrigal Road on 27 December last year. I don't know if I'll ever get my head around it. To the defendant—I sincerely hope you never have to go through sorrow like this, but I also hope that you never again cause anyone else such sorrow.

•

Making the judge cry

Afterwards, the prosecutor let me know there would be journalists on the steps as we left the court complex, and that I didn't have to talk to them unless I wanted to. I'd said most of what I needed to in the courtroom. The only point left to make was an obvious one about cars and their capacity to become death-machines.

Out on the court steps, I resisted the instinctive urge to smile at the camera. I thought about Lindy Chamberlain, and wondered if I'd been naïve choosing to do this. How much grief was enough? What was my face supposed to look like? The grinding grief was suddenly elusive, and instead I felt a strange elation, like the relief when your ears pop as the plane goes up and the pressure equalises in your head. At the very moment my sadness was to be publicly broadcast, I felt lighter—almost fraudulent for making such a fuss. But I held Z's photo inside the envelope and thought, 'She's worth making a fuss over.'

22

Close up with hope

All through 2010, the calendar mocked me. We lived in the shadow of two ghost calendars—the year before, when we'd been unbroken, and the year that might have been. February, the month Haloumi would have been born. June, the birthday that was my first as a mother, but spent without my baby. The June before, I'd just done a pregnancy test and, for the first time ever, encountered that second faint blue line. We went out dancing with friends, and I surreptitiously sipped soft drink, and Rima and I exchanged secret (or probably not so secret) goofy smiles. September 2009, we'd started telling people, and I had trouble doing up my jeans. By November 2009, I was well and truly showing, and my students and colleagues were getting excited for us. November 2010 was a very different story. The criminal proceedings were over and the young man who'd set the billiard balls rolling was in jail, but our daughter was no less dead. We were still having no luck trying to conceive, and the black hole of 27 December was looming.

And then, two weeks after the media bubble that surrounded the sentencing hearing, I was driving somewhere, and while we were waiting to turn right, a silver four-wheel drive turning left swung wide and nearly hit us, but corrected in time. I saw the driver's face—he was young, maybe still on his L-plates—his own eyes as scared as mine.

In the choking tears that followed, I felt a weird confusion. How could this be as terrifying as the moments leading up to our accident, when there was no impact? I knew I was safe this time, but my body and mind remained tensed for the impact, my jaw locked.

The days after were panicky, with headaches and jaw pain from grinding my teeth in my sleep. Another trip to Sydney for an insemination left me wiped out and weepy. I had gone back to full-time work within a few months of the accident, but suddenly I couldn't hold things together anymore. I took sick leave, begged work colleagues to finish some of my marking and cancelled giving a paper at a local conference.

Thursday, 16 December 2010

There is a new sensation I've discovered in the past few months, which I've nicknamed 'the hard swallow'. It happens when I'm driving, and see a four-wheel drive coming towards me, or when I see a baby and try to estimate—11 or 12 months old? Or when the IVF administrator tells me the dollar amount we have to pay to start IVF. A ball of fear or sadness, or something of a similar texture, rises in my throat and I have the urge to run, scream and hide. But I know I can't, so instead I swallow it down, and get on with the business of moving through the world.

I'm not pregnant this time. I didn't really think I was, but when I got to the 27 day mark, I just started entertaining little thoughts, 'maybe Christmas would feel good after all' etc. But no. And while IVF felt like a relatively positive Plan B when I went to visit Dr Lovely last week, it doesn't feel like such a fun path now.

I'm a big hippy, you see. I don't like the idea of doctors taking control of my cycle, forcing my ovaries to blister with artificially stimulated ova, vacuuming out my eggs, and coercing them to germinate with a selected sperm. It all feels a bit too much like high school dancing classes where we were supposed to hold our dancing partner tight enough so that a vinyl record put between us couldn't fall to the floor. It's as though doctors are telling my body, 'Oh, just get out of the way and let us do this properly!' I know what it feels like to have medical experts take over my most basic bodily functions—I'm lucky they did, otherwise I would be dead, but that doesn't mean I like it.

We don't *have* to do IVF. As a dear friend has pointed out, our lack of luck so far is probably more about timing than anything else. But given our issues with frozen inseminations, and the difficulty and stress involved in travelling interstate every month for fresh inseminations, and 'advancing maternal age', it is making sense. What I don't like most about IVF is that I feel corralled into it by fear—fear that maybe Z will be the only baby I have, that it is all too late, that if Christmas 2011 were to roll around without a pregnancy in sight, I'd lose what scrap of sanity I've got left. So it is a pragmatic choice, but a very reluctant, sulky one. And it makes me even sulkier to know how much we have to pay for procedures which I don't want anyway (or wish I didn't need). But this is where the hard swallow comes in.

•

Christmas in Melbourne minus a pregnancy, however, felt too big and too hard to swallow, so we hatched a plan to run away from the whole thing. Like Max in Maurice Sendak's picture book, we would sail off to rumpus with the wild things, or at least, with some friendly wombats. We packed up the car with tents, bags and the girls, drove onto the ferry to Tasmania and sailed off to rumpus with the wombats. And what about the small matter of 27 December—the date that had been hovering like a four-wheel drive half a second before impact? I wanted to look into its beady eyes and remember what it felt like on the other side; to feel whole and unharmed and hopeful. I wanted a whole day where we didn't need to get in the car, preferably with a beach and a big, salty ocean nearby.

Close up with hope

We woke up on Christmas morning in a tiny cabin near Cradle Mountain, and marked the day with small presents, a big walk, and a fancy lunch at the lodge. By 27 December, we were camped near Wineglass Bay. I had been so scared of the day itself, but in the end, it was just an ordinary day—arguments, half-successful pancakes, a picnic lunch, peacemaking. We walked all the way from our campsite to Wineglass Bay and back again (with swimming in between), Rima insisting that we stop at the bar in the lodge for a drink in Z's honour. A superb blue wren joined us on the balcony.

It was almost dusk as we walked back to our campsite via the beach, and in the wet sand, the girls drew our family—depicting Z still in my belly. I wrote her name too, with a Zorro-like 'Z' right at the edge of the waves, where the sand is not solid or liquid but some other matter. The thought that her name would wash away felt like some kind of anti-memorial. Rather than her name persisting, set in stone, it would merge with the grains of sand, with the gallons of ocean and with the movement between them.

•

Tuesday, 11 January 2011

Recently, I've started feeling queasy about my own hope in the same way that I do with really corny advertising. It doesn't feel true. I know from experience that hopes can be shattered, even when you are being cagey, trying not to hope too much. I know at some level, that was why I hadn't finalised a name for Haloumi before she was born, why I hadn't found out her sex. I was trying to arm myself against hope. But I still believed in it—and attempting to guard against it was really just replacing overt hope with secret hope.

I've gone through life with a naïve idea that things will work out, that if I'm calm and careful, it will all be okay. In that moment when the car stopped moving after the impact, when people had arrived on the scene and were helping us, when I'd been able to wriggle my toes, and didn't feel any pain in my uterus, I was so certain that Haloumi would be okay. I was good, I stayed calm, I did everything I could to cooperate with the paramedics and firefighters. I didn't even let the idea that she'd died enter my head—I kept my hand there, on my belly, inconveniencing all the doctors and nurses wielding Dopplers and ultrasound wands, because I was trying to keep her alive by hope alone.

And I was so so wrong—she was so so dead, even by the time they got me in the ambulance. That doesn't mean that screaming and losing it would have been a better response—but it has taken me a long time to try to get my head around my own broken hope. I know it makes no sense, but I'm so sad that my hope wasn't strong enough to save her, that it failed when put to the test.

So, I'm exploring a bit about hope, and Pema Chödrön's suggestion—'if we're willing to give up hope that insecurity and pain can be exterminated, then we can have the courage to relax with the groundlessness of our situation'.[1] That sounds quite stark, but I know very well now that there are no guarantees, that the ground can fall out from under you at any moment. This approach is realistic at least—there really is no hope that you could live your life with nothing bad ever happening to you. But is it a healthy approach to take? Wouldn't it be morbid and negative to be continually mindful of your complete lack of any security? It seems counter-instinctive that you could be both thinking about your 'groundlessness' and 'relaxing' at the same time. So far, though, trying out this groundlessness has been calming in an odd way. It is helping me drive the panics back a bit—or rather to acknowledge them and sit with them rather than run around looking for something I hope might 'make it better'.

But I still find it very hard to embrace the idea that giving up hope is a good thing to do—or that it is a part of appreciating that life is full of impermanence and change. I like hope! I'm always hoping this, hoping that—for myself and for others I care about. So much of the culture I have grown up in is based on the idea that 'things will get better', that the good life is normal. But there is also a big sense of relief in accepting that what happened to us wasn't an aberration from the happy life that everyone else gets—that as sad as it was, loss, injury and grief are part of the human condition. Yes, there are heart-achingly beautiful, good things in the world, but they don't last forever, and death and cancer, and embarrassment and disappointment are just as normal and as common.

This bit especially made sense to me: 'Hope and fear come from feeling that we lack something; they come from a sense of poverty. We can't simply relax with ourselves. We hold onto hope, and hope robs us of the present moment ... Rather than letting our negativity get the better of us, we could acknowledge that right now we feel like a piece of shit and not be squeamish about taking a good look ...'[2]

Now that I've started giving myself the tiny injections of the IVF drugs every morning, like DIY acupuncture, I know that we're getting close to the extreme hope-dance that is an egg pick-up, an embryo-transfer. I haven't coped very well with hope for the last three cycles of inseminations. So I'm going to try this groundlessness—to sit with the complete uncertainty at the heart of baby-making and do a bit less grabbing onto the hope of some other future moment making things better. Of course I want it to work. But I'm curious about how different things might feel if I just take each moment for the groundless, uncertain thing that it is.

Fear is the other one I've been experimenting with, trying to get close up with. On the first day of our holiday, we went white water rafting, and half an hour in, our guide pulled into a deep, still corner of the river, and pointed up. 'See that little cliff?' he said, grinning. 'You're going to jump off that.' And we did. I felt the panic grip me and tell me to turn around, and I hesitated once, well, twice. But then I jumped, and the panic jumped with me and I screamed like a big girl and flapped my arms all the way down. The girls laughed their heads off. And I got to know my fear a little better.

23

The charnel ground

With the intensity of the first anniversary of our accident behind us, January felt like a relief. I would still look at the date and know that a year ago on that day, I was transferred from ICU to the trauma ward, or transferred home from rehab, but these were dates I was familiar with, here on the 'after' side of the river.

I'd decided to sign up to staff one of the January camps held at Somers, where Z's ashes were buried in the bush chapel—partly (if I were honest) to spend some time near her. We were starting our first IVF cycle, and I would wake up early with the summer sunrise, swab my soft belly with alcohol and watch the needle push against my skin, then pop through. It felt momentous. I'd had so many objections to IVF, to the artificiality of it—making your ovaries swell up like cantaloupes, only to be, yes, harvested. But months of flying back and forth to Sydney to meet our donor to conduct inseminations (or asking him to fly down to Melbourne) had been complicated and ultimately fruitless, and I was terrified at the thought of another Christmas with no living baby.

Most mornings, I snuck out to the beach and to Z's spot, to touch the sandy earth and bring her a little flower or a washed-up shark egg. And, after all the rushing about of the past year, it felt like I finally had time to think properly, with a good beach to do it on.

The charnel ground

•

One of the things I had found hard about the idea of being 'in the moment' was the fact that some moments are awful. If you completely focused on that particular moment, wouldn't you drown in the sheer awfulness of it? Wouldn't it be too depressing to survive it? Wasn't it better to just edit those moments out? I had one particular opportunity to test run this theory, because there was quite clearly one moment I would have loved to cut away from the fabric of my life—the moment of impact and everything it set in motion. It couldn't be undone, I understood that, but was it really a moment to focus on?

What if I had taken that moment, where I was sitting in the wreckage—trapped, bleeding and so afraid that the car next to us would explode—and let my fears and hopes dissolve, so that I was no longer being tugged forwards into a better or worse imagined future? What might I have experienced right there? With hindsight, I could have been present for the last moments of my daughter's life. She was doing the hard work of dying while I was fervently wishing I were somewhere else: in an imaginary future where she was okay.

When Rima tried to call me into the moment and asked me, 'Can you feel Haloumi moving?', I was so angry. I stubbornly wanted to avert my attention, to avoid the uncertainty. I look at this now with tenderness. It was a futile denial, like when a cranky three year old holds their hand up so they can't see you. I didn't want to be engulfed by fear, but I couldn't imagine doing anything other than fearing or hoping. I couldn't imagine that I could just sit with the huge, frightening uncertainty of the situation; that I could treasure a moment with my daughter when it was possibly her last.

I thought that by denying the possibility she might die, I could magically save her by force of hope alone. I know there is no way I could really have known what was happening with her, but I wished I'd been a bit more present for those last little beats of her heart. Instead I was demanding something of her she could no longer do.

(*Please, Haloumi, please be okay. Please be okay, my little one.*) I'd sworn off regret, because I didn't think dragging myself into the past helped either, but perhaps there was something in this idea that even the worst moments deserve attention.

It seemed odd to me that such an awful, traumatic moment could also be such a precious one. But it rings true with my other experiences—with the preciousness of seeing her little, still face, and the pride I felt in labouring for her. And, bizarrely, this realisation that paying attention to a moment couldn't make it any worse—and, indeed, that running away from it (into fear, hope or denial) could cause further suffering—made me feel calmer in my grief. I finally felt as though I were learning something from all this grief: that I didn't have to keep grasping for some kind of solution; that I could sit with this discomfort and uncertainty; that I could feel something impossibly painful and still experience it, be alive to it.

On the last night of the camp, all three hundred or so of us filed into the darkness of the bush chapel, and, with the native creatures noisily putting themselves to bed around us, I held a torch and told my story.

> This is my daughter's first big camp. She's not in any of the grouper huts, or in the staff huts or tents. She's here, in the bush chapel—her ashes are buried just between the altar and the bush.
>
> I was eight months pregnant with her when we had a head-on collision with a Pajero. She died on impact from a placental abruption. Apart from that, she was a beautiful, healthy baby with a tiny bruise on her right eyebrow. I was hospitalised for three weeks with a broken knee, broken sternum, lacerations to my liver and spleen and various cuts to my legs, arms and head.
>
> In the last year since the accident, I have had to do the impossible every day. I have planned my baby's funeral from an intensive care bed. I have learned how to walk with a broken knee. I have held the people I love the most while their hearts are breaking and there was nothing I could do to fix it. And every day, I live, while she is dead.

The charnel ground

For a long time I was desperate to escape my grief—I thought there would be some 'solution' to it, a time when I might feel some ground under my feet again. But like it or not, this is the nature of being a human being. We know that we are fragile, and we know that we will all die, but it all seems pretty theoretical until you lose someone you love. It seems impossibly cruel that a baby could die when we loved her so much and we hadn't even had a chance to see her open her eyes. But, this is what life throws at us—impossible miracles like babies, and impossible losses.

And while I now know there are no guarantees, this is what gives me a little peace—that what we have experienced is not a terrible aberration from the good life that we are all entitled to, but that the sadness and wretchedness of grief is part and parcel of the love and inspiration I still feel for my daughter.

I have been reading *When Things Fall Apart* by a Buddhist nun called Pema Chödrön who puts it this way: 'Inspiration and wretchedness are inseparable. We always want to get rid of misery rather than see how it works together with joy. The point isn't to cultivate one thing as opposed to another, but to relate properly to where we are.

'Inspiration and wretchedness complement one another. With only inspiration, we become arrogant. With only wretchedness, we lose our vision. Feeling inspired cheers us up, makes us realise how vast and wonderful our world is. Feeling wretched humbles us. The gloriousness of our inspiration connects us with the sacred elements of the world. But when the tables are turned and we feel wretched, that softens us up. It ripens our hearts. It becomes the ground for understanding others.'

And this is the strange thing. As this loss has carved my heart out so painfully, I've also felt an intensity of joy beyond anything I felt before—often mingled together. Where I thought this pain would crush me, it has transformed me, and by feeling it, and gently observing it, rather than trying to escape it, my heart has expanded beyond my imagination.

It was a relief to let the words out, to make visible my grief. It was all true—there was a new intensity to everything. It was like the rawness where my knee had healed up; the nerves were still not quite sure what messages to send, so they sent them all in loud capitals. As much as I wanted to be okay with the awful moment, to 'lean into the sharp points', as Chödrön would say, I still wanted to transform it into something, to make it worthwhile—to tack on a happy ending. Hope still had its hooks in me.

•

In January 2011, I flew to Cairns to visit my mum. It was as hot as Melbourne but stickier. The first night I slept in Mum's swag outside her campervan, an arc of tent pole holding the mosquito netting away from my face. At one point in the night, a possum investigating my bed woke me up. I fumbled with my tiny torch—I was pretty sure it was a possum. All the same, the next night I slept alongside Mum above her campervan's cab.

I was still reading Pema Chödrön and was struck by her description of the hospital emergency room as the 'closest thing to a charnel ground in our world'.[1] I had a vague, gory idea of what a charnel ground was—a place where human bodies were left to decompose—but it made a weird sort of sense that a charnel ground would be an ideal place to meditate on the nature of death and impermanence. Indeed, it felt like my body had been the charnel ground—housing the dead, being sliced open, pieces of chipped bone and fluids being discarded. So many people, laying their hands on me, holding me together, slicing me up; gory and sacred all at once.

Jen, one of my midwives, had visited us at home in Preston a few weeks after I was released from rehab. She wasn't there in any official capacity, just to say hello and pick up the plastic container that she'd given me in the trauma ward, complete with its big wedge of home-made rhubarb and strawberry cheesecake.

The charnel ground

'You're looking good,' she said, coming onto the verandah.

'Much better than when we met in the ER, I bet,' I said.

'Yeah. You were looking very grey for a while there; you'd lost a lot of blood.'

'From the liver and spleen?'

'Maybe, but I think it was mostly from the abruption. When the surgeon did the incision for the C-section, there was blood everywhere …' She winced and smiled. 'On the walls, on us—bit of a horror-movie scene!'

And we laughed, because this was my squeamish body producing horror-movie effects that made seasoned midwives wince. Yet, her reaction was not horror or disgust for my charnel ground of a body—just a pragmatic bearing witness, a tenderness.

24
Fat Tuesday

While I continued the IVF injections and my ovaries swelled, Tropical Cyclone Yasi was building in the Pacific Ocean off Fiji. As Yasi neared the Queenland coast, and shifted direction towards Cairns, where my mum, brother and sister-in-law were living, it was upgraded from category 3 to 4 and then to 5, putting it in the ranks of Hurricane Katrina. I'd just finished reading *Zeitoun*, by Dave Eggers, about one family's experience of the chaos that was Katrina, and I was terrified. Mum was holed up with my brother and sister-in-law in their Cairns apartment; thankfully, in a cyclone-proof building. They loaded mattresses against the windows, and were well stocked with food and water.

When text messages came through, letting us know that they were okay, I could finally exhale. The storm had been noisy, but not as destructive as had been feared, at least in Cairns. Between them, my mother and brother had survived four car crashes, the Black Saturday bushfires, a Bolivian uprising, and now, a tropical cyclone, the lucky buggers.

Whether it was the IVF hormones or general cyclone anxiety, I still felt off-balance and tender, with a weird low-level nausea. If my ovaries made noises, they would have been submarine-depth-sounding 'pings'.

So, it was a further relief when the clinic rang after a scan to say they were scheduling me for an egg retrieval.

Our egg pick-up was on a Friday. I slipped so easily back into patient mode; *Here, you drive.* I surfaced from the sedation in a recovery room, alongside two other women. A nurse came along to see how we were, whispered in each of our ears the results of the egg retrieval—it felt very *The Handmaid's Tale*. They'd harvested an even dozen of my eggs, whisked away to be firmly introduced to their spermy boyfriends. I was reunited with Rima in the waiting room, wearing a groggy smile, and hugged her with what felt like big, fuzzy gloves, and spent the rest of the day at home under a doona, half-watching the midday movie.

We were back at the clinic two days later, for the embryo transfer. No sedation this time, just the waking indignity of chatting while the doctor navigated a fine catheter through my cervix. The embryologist appeared, and asked us to confirm our names and the name of our donor, and we saw on the screen a magnified blob: two plump cells within a circular cell wall. *Welcome aboard, tiny speck!*

•

In the quiet waiting space, we took a daytrip down to Somers to visit Z and the bush chapel. It was a whole year now since we'd farewelled Z's gritty ashes into a sandy hole. We took her some baby roses from the front garden, listened to the birds and the crash of waves, and let the dogs run on the beach.

The ten days before any pregnancy could possibly be detected inched past. I dreamt that I was driving but I couldn't see properly, that I drove a truck off a cliff, that we survived and stole towels from a great aunt. The first home pregnancy test was negative. I was deflated, but held out a little hope that I'd just tested too early. But then, a day later, my period arrived and I felt silly for believing that such a tiny thing could actually turn into a baby. I was sulky about turning up to the clinic for the official blood test. What was the point, when it was so clearly going to be negative?

Except that it wasn't. The test came back with a HCG of thirty-seven—a fraction of the 2063 I'd had with Z, but, still, a positive. 'Come back on Tuesday,' said the nurse over the phone. 'I'm sorry; it is really just too early to tell as yet.'

On Tuesday, my HCG level was seventy-eight; still very sluggish and probably an indicator of an implantation, then early miscarriage, explained the nurse. 'Come back on Friday—but if you get any sharp abdominal pains, go straight to emergency, just in case it's ectopic.'

Friday, 25 February 2011

When I arrive at the clinic for my blood test this morning it hasn't opened yet. A queue of people stretches a good fifteen metres down the hallway. Usually we only cross paths in ones and twos in the waiting room. We glance at one another and drop our gaze, respectful of our mutual privacy; we studiously read trashy magazines.

But here we all are, leaning against the wall, relieved and embarrassed to see just how many of us there are. Some women are alone, but most are accompanied by a male partner. 'Here to support her' are the looks they give one another, not so much 'I just want to be a dad'. Either way, they move sheepishly when the queue starts to advance. We didn't giggle about this type of baby-making in high school.

Seated in the waiting room, I start reading a newspaper article about the Christchurch earthquakes. An earthquake begins in me, sobs catching in my ribs, tears steaming to the surface. I want to close the paper, to stop all these sad things from happening, to un-read the headline, 'Mother dies with baby in her arms'. I try to divert, read something else. But still, my body freezes, remembers the sensation of being pinned by twisted metal, the realisation that

I can't get out on my own, someone has to come and help me. This fear is here even without the newspaper. I take a deep breath and open the flimsy pages again and let myself weep for the mother, for her baby, and for me and my baby. All that sadness muddied together—if I could just breathe it all in, soak it all up and breathe out a sense that it will all be okay, that there is something connecting my child and I that cannot be crushed by a falling building or by the impact of a 4-wheel drive.

•

On Friday, my hCG level was up to 201. This time, I got the call from the specialist early pregnancy nurse. She asked me again about the bleeding. I explained that it had been heavy, like a normal period. That it had stopped now.

The nurse hmphed.

'It's clear that there's been implantation, and that you've got pregnancy hormones being produced; it's just that those levels are much lower than we'd like to see. You'll just have to come back on Monday morning for another blood test.'

'So, have you ever seen a viable pregnancy with those kinds of numbers?'

'I have, but it's important to be realistic about your chances here—realistically, it is looking very unlikely at this stage.'

I put down the phone and felt like laughing out loud. *Ha ha.* Realistic! The realistic view was that they had no idea what was happening, and neither did I. We were all spectators to the unfolding soap opera that was my uterine environment.

By Sunday night, though, my Zen was running out. I had fretful dreams of dodgy hotels, where one room connected to another and another and another. I kept waking, thinking it was time to get up and go in for my blood test, even though it was 3 a.m., 4 a.m., 5 a.m. I'd run my situation past my online IVF veteran friends, and heard story after story of low HCG results that were now snoring happily in the cot down the hall. A little speck of hope had got under my skin, and with it, the fear that it would be dashed.

By the Monday morning, my HCG had risen to 630. And although it was the same Nurse Realistic giving me the news, she was much more upbeat this time. She'd spoken with my doctor, and he didn't see any need for a further blood test, just a scan in a week's time.

'So, this might mean that it may actually be viable?'

There was a big, realistic intake of breath. 'Look. With all early pregnancies, but especially when your betas started low, we can't really confirm anything until the scan; but, yes, congratulations. But if you do have any sharp pains or bleeding, don't ignore it, go straight to emergency.'

I couldn't help it—underneath all the caveats, the one word I heard was 'congratulations'. *Welcome, uncertainty—come on in.*

A week earlier, when I'd been certain I wasn't pregnant, I had booked a flight up to Sydney as a consolation prize. I could catch up with friends, enjoy the Gay and Lesbian Mardi Gras parade, and if the timing was right, attempt a fresh insemination with our donor. But now, the trip was a welcome distraction while I waited out the days until the next scan.

Sydney, when I touched down, was thick with memories of 'before'. They were heavy on the ground and mostly still undisturbed because I had spent so little time there since December 2009. The sight of kids in the uniforms from the girls' old school, the shops where I had bought ordinary, inconsequential things, the road that led to our house—all of these things couldn't fade into the background until my brain had trotted through its 'Last time I saw x, Haloumi was here' routine.

I returned to one of my favourite Sydney spots: the women's baths at Coogee. The last time I was there, my Haloumi-filled belly had stuck out obscenely between my bikini top and bottom. I had greeted other swimmers with my stretch marks. That belly was remarkable. Everyone remarked on it, speculated on Haloumi's gender and wished me well.

Fat Tuesday

I had so many pregnant and unpregnant swims there over the years. Some involved mildly athletic laps; some, snorkelling and marvelling at the starfish, shellfish and, once, even an octopus under the surface; some were splashy and noisy, with the girls; some quiet and contemplative, with no one else in the water. I'd seen it in a storm, with the waves crashing over the rock wall; I'd seen the surface sparkle with a beating sun; and I'd eyed off the greeny-blue depths when it was far too cold to swim.

And now—who knows? I was egging on this tiny speck of potential, hoping it was in the right spot, hoping it wasn't ectopic, chemical, blighted, all kinds of words for 'lost already'. To swim there felt like an act of love—towards my tentative self and this little question mark of cells.

I met up with an old friend who had also been going through IVF, and was now ten weeks pregnant, that odd early stage of pregnancy where you just feel fat and off-colour; a tenuous, uncertain state. We arranged a spot in the mardi gras parade on my usual float. I'd been to the workshop earlier that day, and made loopy green headdresses and tutus for us. And we danced all the way up Oxford Street, spangled with glitter and shining from the cheers of the crowd. I dared to imagine two small children who might delight in the idea they'd marched in the mardi gras even before they were born. It was our Fat Tuesday (quite literally; from the French, *mardi gras*)—we feasted on hope while we could.

Flying back to Melbourne, that hope solidified a little. Just being around someone else in those strange early days of pregnancy made me feel like maybe, maybe, we'd see a heartbeat too this time. Lo and behold, at the scan on Monday, there was a fetal sac in the uterus, where it should have been, but nothing else. No fetal pole, no heartbeat.

Our doctor was philosophical. 'There are a number of possibilities here. It could be that you've just got a slow starter. Sometimes embryos drop a few cells before implanting, and that puts them a little behind. It's still early days, so I think we need another scan, next week, before we make a call either way.'

On the Tuesday, I was back at work, wearing a summery outfit—new dress, new shoes—when the bleeding started. There was a heaviness, but it came suddenly, like something loosening. In the time it took for me to half-run from my office to the toilet, my new strappy white sandals and the lino floor were marked with big polka dots of blood, perfectly circular.

25

Undone

In the emergency waiting room at the Women's, we ran into my friend Sophie, tall as always, but rounder than usual. She was coming in with her partner for her 38-week check-up. Soph had been at the picnic on the day of our accident. She had just been starting IVF, and there I was, heavily, smugly pregnant. When we said our goodbyes, I gave her a hug and said, 'Good luck!' She squeezed me back and smiled, 'You too!' And as I'd walked to the car, I thought, 'I don't need luck, I'm already there.' How these little memories mocked me. Now, it was the best I could do to acknowledge Sophie and indicate that we couldn't really talk.

The hospital took bloods and let us wait around for the results. My hCG levels were still rising, but we'd need a scan to get any real information on what this bleeding meant.

We went to our fertility clinic the next morning, and, despite the horror-movie bleeding, the scan showed that the little fetal sac was still there. There was still no sign of a fetal pole but the sac was persisting nonetheless. When we went back four days later and saw the same sight on the ultrasound screen—no growth, no embryo—our doctor was pragmatic. 'Looks like nothing is going to happen with this one; I'm sorry. I can book you in for a D&C on Friday, if that suits?'

I wanted to be just as pragmatic. I would work, as planned, on Wednesday and Thursday, then go in for the D&C on Friday. Miscarriage managed—a Harry Potter-esque tap of a wand and the slate (uterus?) would be wiped clean. *This is just a blip*, I told myself. *We will get there.*

That Wednesday morning, I forced myself into some clothes and out the door. I was too shaky to drive, so I took the tram, hoping that none of my students would see me sobbing behind my sunglasses. By the time I reached work, my tears had crystallised into a hard, mean anger. Walking to my building from the tram stop, I slammed each foot down. I deliberately grazed my knuckles against walls. I locked myself in the bathroom, and wept against the wall, tapping and then knocking my forehead against the bricks. While my head was screaming expletives, there was another voice there too; the one I would speak to Z in when I looked up at her star, or leaned in close to open roses and breathed them in. *Oh, honey, this is so hard.* It was that voice that stopped me from punching the wall, that gently took me back outside so I could retrace my steps, get back on the tram, walk home and get into bed, send an email to my colleague that I wouldn't be able to teach the next day, that I was having a miscarriage. Today there would be no forward motion. This pregnancy had to be unravelled before we could go on; things were not just paused, but would have to go in reverse for a while.

My colleague responded compassionately. 'Take this week and next week off,' she urged. I did that, and, instead of booking in for the D&C, called up my doctor's office and asked for recommendations of where to go for the less interventionist medical version. Part of that white-hot anger, I'd discovered when I took the time to listen to it, was anger with myself, for thinking that I could just timetable my grief around my work responsibilities. But the whitest white-hot anger focused on the planned procedure on Friday and the thought of more surgery, more prodding. I had handed my body over to the IVF people so many times already. I'd never wanted a C-section, I'd never wanted to go through IVF, and the thought of more surgery triggered a kind of roar within me of *Leave me alone!* I was furious that my body couldn't just sort this out on its own; yet, I still wanted to defend this small bit of turf, to retain some kind of control.

After a few hours, I heard back from our IVF doctor. Yes, a medical termination was probably possible, but you needed to be specially registered in order to prescribe it, and he wasn't. He gave me the name of another provider, and I drove for an hour to find myself in a dodgy-looking carpark with vague signage, and, soon after that, a dingy waiting room full of brochures about 'options'.

So this was what an abortion clinic looked like. It was a far cry from the soft lighting and tasteful art that decorated the IVF clinic where this pregnancy had started. The accusing fingers of the anti-abortion lobby had marked out pregnancy termination care as something controversial and distasteful—in the process, stigmatising the women who needed these services and the health professionals who provided them. Services like this were construed as the exact opposite of the optimistic health business of making people well and delivering living babies. Yet, here I was, straddling those categories—desperate for a living child, but needing help to evict a pregnancy.

This doctor wasn't used to seeing people who wanted to be pregnant. When I asked if he was sure that the pregnancy wasn't viable, he said, 'I don't know—if you're not ready, wait a week and have another scan.' I chickened out and drove home, cursing and crying at the thought of another week's purgatory.

At home, I spoke to a midwife friend, who informed me that the Women's Hospital could admit me as a day patient for 'medical management of miscarriage'. I called their clinic, and when I went in for another scan, we saw the same little heartbeatless oval floating there. 'Come back tomorrow,' they said, 'at 7 a.m.'

I took comfortable clothes and a good book. After they'd given me the medicine, I stared earnestly out the window. *Little one, it's okay to go now. I know, you tried so hard, it wasn't your fault that things didn't work out. It's okay, little one.* This time, when I bled, I was relieved rather than scared. I didn't want to be unconscious for this. I needed to be there to know for myself that it was over. When the pains became bad, the nurses gave me some pethidine, and, when it was all over, a cup of tea.

•

On the Monday morning after my hospital visit, Rima was driving me to work when my phone rang. It was one of the pathologists from the Women's. They'd tested the 'products of conception' from the miscarriage and there was a chance it might have been a molar pregnancy, a disorder with the placenta. 'We don't know yet whether it was molar, but testing will take about four weeks, so it's a good idea to make sure you don't get pregnant in the meantime.' No chance of that, I assured her.

At work, I googled 'molar pregnancy'; the Women's Hospital had a helpful fact sheet. This type of pregnancy involved a genetic defect with the embryo, which meant that it was all placenta, no baby. And worse, in a science-fiction twist, sometimes it could develop into a mole-like growth that burrows into your uterus, cells dividing and multiplying and, all the while, pumping out more and more of the hCG hormones that make blue lines blithely appear on pregnancy tests. Undetected, a malignant molar pregnancy could become cancerous and spread to other organs, though it apparently responded well to chemotherapy.

'Chemotherapy'. This was not a word I was expecting to come across in the process of trying to get pregnant. I took deep breaths, and made a cup of tea. 'All they're doing is further testing. And the results will take four weeks. The most likely outcome is that I don't have this.' *Exhale*. I would worry about this if and when I was diagnosed. In the meantime, I had work to do.

On the Thursday, I was working from home. There was a staff seminar scheduled for lunchtime that I would go in for but, meanwhile, I had teaching prep to do. My 'work space' wasn't ideal. The secretaire in the hallway had a small drop-down desk, so I sat there, on a folding chair. The doorbell rang, and it was the postie holding an enormous brown-paper parcel the size of a small TV. I wasn't expecting anything, so my heart lifted a little—I thought it might be from a friend. The label was typed, though, and the parcel wasn't nearly as heavy as its size suggested. When I tore away the paper, I discovered first one empty 4-litre plastic bottle with a medical patient ID label; then another; then two more, along with a heavy letter from the Women's Hospital. It was addressed to me, but was a form letter referring to my 'recent diagnosis' of a molar pregnancy.

Here was a helpful pamphlet on the different kinds of molar pregnancies. Here was a flyer for the molar pregnancy support group. Here were detailed instructions on how to collect all your urine in one of the 4-litre containers over a twenty-four-hour period, and a little map showing the location of the hospital pathology unit where the samples needed to be dropped off within twenty-four hours—one each week. I had visions of wandering nonchalantly through the hospital sliding doors, lugging a sloshing container of my own wee. I backtracked to the letter—*diagnosis*? 'What? I'd only had the call from the hospital pathologist a few days ago. I thought it was going to take four weeks to get a result?'

My stomach dropped. I frantically dialled the number on the letter. I needed to sort this out—had I been diagnosed? The first number led me to an answering machine, as did the next two, so I tried going through the switchboard and searching the hospital website for clues. An hour later, I was none the wiser but flicked back into my email account to discover an increasingly frantic series of emails from the co-convenor of the seminar series.

The seminar. The floor suddenly seemed unsteady beneath me. I'd completely forgotten about the seminar, leaving my co-convenor to somehow locate the guest speaker and chair the event in my place. I called and left a breathless message, apologising for not being there and letting her know that I'd had some upsetting medical news.

I didn't hear anything until I received an email from my head of school, indicating that my colleague had spoken to her about my worrying news, and that they had decided to employ a casual to cover my teaching for the rest of the semester. For the third time in one day, things crumbled beneath my feet, but this time I had an overwhelming sense of shame and stupidity. They were collapsing not because of a medical problem, or an administrative error. This was a crumbling I had created directly, from my own blind panic. I wanted to disappear, to shrink into a tiny ball and roll underneath the couch. Yet there was also a small, burning fury with myself and the situation. I wanted this job, I didn't want to be sidelined.

•

Despite the cool autumn morning, I was in the sweat of an energised panic when I arrived at work just after 8 a.m. the next day. The afternoon before, I'd done what I could to repair the damage, and had set up a 9 a.m. meeting with my boss, to plead my case to continue teaching for the semester.

I'd slept fitfully, resisting further consultations with Dr Google on molar pregnancies and what they could mean, and furious with myself for taking my work for granted, for letting these medical dramas cloud my work. Where my body had felt slowed for weeks, as the possibility of the new pregnancy leached out of me, now I was suddenly taut with tension. Nothing concentrates the mind like threat.

I bounced up the lino steps two at a time, silently punching out the lines of my reasonable email to my boss from the afternoon before. As I touched my hand to my office door, my mobile rang, and I answered it with the same efficiency. It was Penny.

'You have a nephew!'

'What?'

'You have a nephew—he was born at five-fifteen this morning!'

I let myself into my office, locked the door behind me, and stepped over to the window. 'Oh, Pen, wow … wow.' I looked at the calendar. I knew Penny's due date was any day now—I'd been on stand-by to be there at the birth for her and Kent. 'I'm sorry I wasn't there for the birth—did you call me? Did everything go okay?'

'Yes; it was all too late, and then too quick, to call you. It was intense—the worst bit was being separated from him for an hour while I waited on a trolley for a doctor to come and do some stitches. I was in a hospital gown, and didn't have my glasses, and I think they forgot about me. I had to go wandering up to the nurses' station to see what was happening—half-naked, blind as a bat—and then they sent me back down to the birthing centre for the stitches, anyway.'

'Oh, love; ouch. That's not good. But you're back in the birth centre now? Can I come in and see you? And meet your son—your son—oh, wow. I've got to see my boss at nine, but can I come right after that?'

'Yes, come! Is stuff okay with your boss?'

'Yeah, yeah; it's all okay. I should be there before ten.'

Gratitude rushed over me. He was here, he was okay, and he was a boy. I could love him, and I could congratulate Penny and Kent wholeheartedly, clean of the sadness and conflicted feelings that I feared might have come with a baby girl.

And, despite all my brokenness, I met with my boss, apologised for missing the seminar and negotiated my workload. Then I drove over to the same hospital where we'd had Z's last scan, a few days before the accident, and met my tiny new nephew, awash with love for him and his parents, and the honour of being his Aunty Hannah.

That night, with two seemingly impossible things already under my belt for the day, Rima and I went with friends to a Melbourne Comedy Festival show, and I laughed so hard I bumped my front tooth on the seat in front of me, chipping the cap the dentist had so carefully used to repair my teeth after the accident. My laughter morphed first into sobs at another thing gone wrong, but then into a deeper laughter that stretched the entire space between the utter devastation and sheer ridiculousness of my situation.

26

Tsunami

On Easter Friday 2011, I got a call from V, a mutual friend of Karin and Ned, our friends who had lost their baby son, Albie, just six months after our accident. They were still living in Paris, Karin was pregnant again, and their baby was due any day now.

'Hi, Hannah, just wanting to let you know that Baby Esther was born yesterday,' said V. Before I could squeak my congratulations, she added, 'It's not good news, though, I'm afraid.'

'Oh.' My brain started moving in circles—how could this not be good news?

'There was a lot of blood when she was born, and she's needing a lot of help to breathe. It is really not looking good.' V wasn't teary, just solid and serious.

I had a lot of questions. I had so many happier possibilities that I needed to put forward—'Sometimes babies just need some help to start breathing, I guess?'—only for V to gently pack them away.

Karin and Ned's parents were flying to Paris to be there, and to meet baby Esther. Even I could join the dots. They had to meet her while they could, because she was a very ill little baby.

'I'll keep you posted,' said V.

I asked her to pass on my love, and tell Karin and Ned that I was sending all the good thoughts I could muster. I put the phone down and wept.

I dug through my knitting things. I found a silky-feeling navy blue alpaca yarn and a hot pink wool of similar weight, and cast on. I was furious. Furious with myself for tossing our dear friends into the category of those lucky people whose seemingly effortless pregnancies rubbed salt into our own painfully unsuccessful attempts to conceive.

Back in October 2010, in the same week that Karin had told me she was pregnant, two couples in our Thursday night SANDS (Stillbirth and Neonatal Death Support) group had given their own glowing news, along with the ongoing trickle of Facebook announcements. I'd started to think my psychologist was also pregnant, and, after having to cancel a number of appointments due to illness, she confirmed my suspicions. Penny had also let me know that she was pregnant. Her news stung a little less because she had grieved Z with us. Our loss was hers too, and her news was our good news.

Nonetheless, it was starting to feel as if everyone but us could get pregnant. (Apparently, there is a made-up term for this state of mind: *preganoia*.) I didn't say anything to Karin (how could I?), but in my own head, a small, resentful voice muttered and felt betrayed, as though Karin and Ned had skipped the baby queue. I hadn't wished them ill, but my heart had closed a fraction, and refocused on my own misery.

As my knitting needles worked their way around—pink, navy, pink, navy, pink, navy—they repeated my mantra: *Please let her be okay, please let her be okay, please let her be okay. Please,* I implored all the gods I didn't believe in, and the universe I'd sworn at for the last fifteen months, *please let something biblical happen*—'and on the third day, she breathed on her own, and resumed normal brain activity'.

We spent the long weekend around the house, in a state of suspended animation. I was supposed to be marking essays but found myself staring out the window or reading the same line over and over. I gave up, and just kept knitting.

On Easter Monday, V rang again. 'I'm sorry, it's not good news. They took Esther off life support this morning, and she died in Karin and Ned's arms.'

I shuddered.

'Oh no. Oh, V, no! That is just not bloody fair. For fuck's sake.'

V was quiet. I didn't know how many of these calls she had to make that day, how many times she'd already had to calmly tell this news, to be on the other end of the phone making it real over and over again. I apologised. I asked more questions.

My fingers pressed into the points of my knitting needles, while we touched on funeral plans (they would bring her home, to be buried with her brother). I hung up. The beanie wasn't finished yet. If I'd knitted it faster, would she have lived? If I'd been a good enough friend to have knitted it before she was born, would she have been okay? I was reading Joan Didion, and knew that this was magical thinking, as was my fuzzy presumption that pregnancies and living babies could be doled out on the basis of an orderly queue. But that didn't stop the hypotheticals whizzing faster and faster around my head.

If losing one baby were enough to break you, what would losing two do to you? To survive losing two in a row was inconceivable. But Karin and Ned were not in a lonely category all their own. Of course, there were women like my great-grandmother, who, I knew, had mourned three babies and one six year old—heartbreakingly normal for turn-of-the-nineteenth-century Melbourne. Now, when I looked at the black-and-white photos of her, I saw not just weariness but sorrow and strength. I was dimly aware that women living in other decades and in countries with poorer health systems had much higher infant mortality statistics than ours, but until now I had failed to imagine properly the babies or the mothers embedded in those statistics.

The only other person I then knew to have lost two babies was my friend Jude. In a friend's Newcastle kitchen, she had given me mates' rates haircuts. After our accident, she got in touch on Facebook to offer her condolences and disclosed that she'd lost two babies in a row to stillbirth. Her son and daughter would have been twenty-nine and twenty-eight. She and her then husband lived in a small town at the time, and after the second stillbirth, her husband had to visit all the local shops and tell everyone, so that she could go to the shops without people asking, 'What did you have? Boy or girl?'

More than a year out from losing Z, I was barely hanging on by my fingernails. I tried to extrapolate my loss, to multiply it by two, and then fast forward several decades, but I still couldn't see myself ever becoming as Zen, as kind, or as genuinely funny and cheery as Jude. If I lost another baby, I imagined, I would spontaneously combust. But Karin and Ned didn't combust, and it wasn't for any lack of love or feeling for their children. Their ability to keep breathing, to continue moving through time and space, and even to find the headspace to ask how we were going, blew my mind. 'Freaking superheroes,' I thought. But also beautiful human beings. As Karin and I kept up our correspondence, my desperation to fix things for them, to magically knit it all back together, ebbed away. All I could do was respond, bear witness to their grief, and let the conversation move lightly between picking colours for baby-sized caskets, knitting, funeral arrangements, our ongoing IVF saga, and laughing about weeping on public transport and the horrible realness of burying babies.

Somewhere in those conversations, my idea of a 'fair' or fixed amount of grief and misfortune got washed out to sea. I knew Karin and Ned well. They are two of the most generous, open-hearted and hilarious people I know. If anyone deserved a living child, it was them. The fact that their universe had been destroyed not once but twice was irrefutable proof that life was not fair. My fantasy that there was some kind of balance sheet, or someone out there to add up the columns, was gone, swept away like the fragile bit of debris that it was.

Just six weeks before, we'd watched the 40-metre waves of the Tōhoko tsunami sweep across the Japanese countryside, insensible to the homes, farms, nuclear power plants and 18 000 people in its path. We'd sat agog, awed by the power, the destruction, and, God forbid, the beauty of the ocean. Not only were my fantasies of fairness now dissolved, but also my tenuous idea that we could map everything into categories: good/bad, happy/sad, fair/unfair. It wasn't just the ocean that could be both indescribably beautiful and heartbreakingly destructive, that simultaneously fostered life and wrought suffering and death. When I looked closely, I reluctantly had to put more and more things in that awesome/devastating category: human relationships (including parenting), technology, cars, food, substances, law, democracy, nature—in short, anything that mattered. There was no 'safe' zone, there was no unmediated 'good', just a whole lot of awesome/devastating chaos.

That didn't mean I accepted it all, or that I was indifferent to whether it came out as heads or tails, awesome or devastating, in any particular instant. Of course, I had a preference. Of course, I still prefer peace to war, love to fear, alive to dead, fairness to injustice, friendliness to cruelty, safety to harm. But I recognise these as my preferences, not universal truths.

I would have understood if Karin and Ned had become bitter, with the manifestly unfair hand they'd been dealt. But they didn't. Instead, Karin's mantra was *See beauty, see beauty*. That meant all of it. The devastation, the grief, those short hours of holding our dead babies in our arms, were just as tender and beautiful as the prettier, smoother stuff I'd previously taken as beauty.

27
Earth and sun

Late July 2011 found me in Queensland for a conference. After all the molar pregnancy drama, the tests had come back negative, and I could happily put the 4-litre urine containers in the recycling and move on with IVF. Two unsuccessful frozen embryo transfers later, the grinding greys had returned. There was no date to look forward to in the calendar—we were already throwing everything at Project Bump, and getting nothing back. After refusing to miscarry a 'blighted ovum' in March, my body seemed to have gone into a sulk or lost interest. In May and June, there hadn't been even a whiff of a pregnancy symptom.

Saturday, 23 July 2011

There's a special art to running through crowded city streets. Speed up, sideways step, watch for a gap. My heart expands to knock at my ribs and nearly bowl over the people in my path, until I'm all heart—messy, beating, puffing and suddenly seeing all these messy human hearts around me. A woman sees me running towards her and fear blanks across her face briefly—she looks wildly behind me, her own steps a little quicker. I have a good reason to run—I don't want to be late for my osteo appointment, but I feel like I've just woken, as though my blood is reaching cells that have been slowly greying.

Things have been really grey lately. Everything is a big effort. I'm kind of embarrassed to write about it because this kind of sadness is dull. I bore myself. It's as though I'm stuck at the bottom of a big hole in the ground. Poem by poem, I'm digging myself out, and I know from the voices of loved ones which way is up, but I can't really pretend to be anywhere else at the moment. I have to make reluctant friends with this situation.

So what are you trying to tell me, deep dark hole? To stop dreaming of the stars (and one particularly bright little star)? That my slow-crafted words will come to nothing? That I am one and the same as the slippery grey-black clay on every side of me? Come on, hole, teach me your lesson and then we can be done. I'm not going to be bullied into silence and self-pity. Enough of that.

I'm not at all prejudiced against holes in the ground—in fact, my daughter lives in one, as do many of my favourite trees, earthworms and root vegetables. If dirt is my destiny, then bring it on, dirt. Show me your microbes, let me remember what dirt smells like, let me feel the grit of it between my fingers.

Time moves slowly under the earth. Things are hidden, processes work slowly but powerfully. Minerals are crushed, underground rivers carved, liquids percolate drip by drip, continental plates grind past one another millimetre by millimetre—all monumental changes occurring at a pace measured in centuries rather than minutes. What else is down here? Things unwanted or forgotten, buried and mourned—so many things lost and wasted which are slowly being turned back into the earth itself. Nothing goes away down here, but is slowly transformed, releasing water and nutrients to feed patient tree roots, or our lawn. This is where rivers are born. Nothing flashy or spectacular, just cold humble earth.

Dear hole in the ground, that's what I'd like—some of that persistence, slow elemental momentum. The ability to slowly

Earth and sun

work through this sad stuff with earthworms and use it to grow something good.

•

After tears and long conversations with friends who were IVF veterans, we went back to our doctor with a proposal—to stop the frozen transfers of two-day embryos and start again on a new protocol, of growing the embryos to blastocyst stage (about five days), so that if they made it that far, they'd have a stronger prospect of success. Our doctor was willing, and so we were all set to start a stimulation cycle in July, until I realised that the egg pick-up dates would have conflicted with a conference I'd agreed to speak at. A few months before, frustrated from all the waiting and delays, it would have been unimaginable to put fertility treatment on hold. But now, it felt like a small assertion of control over the process. I was more than just a pincushion; or, at least, I was a pincushion with things in her life other than the IVF process. And as wonderful as it would be to become pregnant again, to try our hand at parenting a living child, I didn't feel the same desperate grasping for it as I had before.

Rima didn't join me on the conference trip, so I was alone in what turned out to be an enormous apartment—and the biggest chunk of solitude I'd had since those weeks in hospital and rehab. The unfamiliar Queensland sun streamed loudly into the bedroom and woke me; a revelation after becoming accustomed to dark Melbourne mornings. I laid a towel on the floor and began a sun salute, relishing the uncluttered space and lifting my face to the morning light.

Even with eyes closed, the light made everything glow. And I missed it when I folded at the hips for *Uttanasana*, to bend my knees and lay my hands flat on the floor on either side of my feet. I felt the sun again when I stepped my right leg back into a lunge, then brought the other leg back and dropped my hips for cobra pose, indulging my face in the sun's warmth; only to miss it again, when I lifted my hips and dropped my head for *adho mukha shavasana* (downward-facing dog). And it occurred to me that this was exactly the pattern of things—alternating between time with your face to the sun, feeling exalted; and time facing the darkness, feeling humbled. Day and night, life and death, love and loss. And my job was not to chase one or the other but to move freely between the two, to honour both and to keep breathing all the while.

•

I had been waiting for a happy ending for this book. I couldn't bear the thought of leaving my story here, in what I'd thought of as the 'waiting place' between one (silent) baby and the next, hopefully more noisy, one. But this 'waiting place' is all I have right now—it's all anyone has when they've lost one baby and are hoping for another. There's no fast-forward button we can push to speed through to the 'good bits'. And even if there were, I'm less and less sure I would have wanted to push it. As painful as this grieving has been, it is mine, and it connects me to my daughter, as well as to everyone else who has suffered loss.

In that dark year after our accident, the thing that made me choke with fear and sadness was the idea of no more Z. I thought, 'That's it. My whole relationship with my daughter was over and done with before it had hardly started.' Thirty-six photos, some inky footprints and handprints, a tiny amount of ashes, and a drop of her blood on a blanket my mum had made; the countable, finite remains of my child. It wasn't enough, it would never be enough. It was such a sad, awful, unfillable hole of 'no more' that, to live in this world, I had to close that drawer, to look elsewhere for the 'more' I needed.

What I hadn't imagined was the feeling of my soul tearing in two as I tried to hurtle away from her. It was an impossible choice: to go back and sit at that point in the road where she disappeared, or to move on. In that linear frame, it was either backwards, towards death and sorrow; or forwards into life and good things, but away from my child.

Specifically, the 'more' that I was looking for was to get pregnant again. I was so sure it would happen. I don't think I had really let go of feeling pregnant. This was my pregnancy and I would finish it, even if I had to mourn a daughter along the way. As I had danced uphill, waving my mardi gras pompoms, tenaciously pregnant, it had felt like forward motion. In spite of everything, I would move on. Now that we were moving, I could feel gracious about the pauses along the road the IVF process had imposed, even though I'd been impatient at the time.

But when I'd unwrapped the parcel from the Women's Hospital, with its generic 'you're diagnosed' letter, something broke in me. I thought, initially, that it was my sanity, that I'd finally popped a crucial cog and I'd be completely broken. But what was broken was my idea of a future without her—a future where that empty space was filled by another, living, baby. A molar pregnancy meant having to wait at least six months to a year before I could try to conceive again. And maybe this wasn't just the pause button; maybe this would mean Z was my only child. Just having to think about that question made me stare very hard at the train tracks while I waited to cross at the level crossing.

The molar pregnancy diagnosis also gave me plenty of time to think. I was scared that if I really looked hard at my grief for Z, if I opened that drawer, the big, sad black hole of 'no more' would suck me in and swallow me whole. Because there was no solution to it. There was no way my logical brain could think a way around the big, stark reality of no more Z.

I had been holding my breath for so long waiting for another baby that I wanted to vehemently push each babyless minute past me and away from me—just throw it away. As long as there was some prospect of another pregnancy to look forward to, I could mark a date in the calendar and set my eyes on it, hold on for that date, even if it were shifting away from me cycle after cycle. But now I no longer had that option; at least until I got the all clear on the molar pregnancy front.

I was furious with myself for being tricked by my own body, with that duplicitous bundle of non-baby cells, and with everyone and everything. I came closer to psychiatric-hospital madness than I ever wanted to come. This was not the quiet, weary disinclination to continue existing that I'd seen in my mum and had glimpses of myself. Instead it was a crackling-hot rage, to smash up myself, my situation and anything in my path. Most of all, what broke was the hoped-for Hannah, who I'd been preparing my life for, who had everything in order but who never seemed to arrive, despite my best efforts. Hoped-for Hannah's baby didn't die, she didn't need IVF, and she could choose when she got pregnant, while managing a glittering career. No wonder she was so infuriating. I had hoped so hard and for so long that to smash up those hopes felt like it would break me. But, in breaking, I also exhaled, and felt what it might be like to live without hope dragging me forwards into an imaginary future moment. Exhausted with my own drama, I lay on the floor with all that sadness, and we breathed and looked at one another. And I breathed in all the scary things that a molar pregnancy might mean: not knowing whether I could get pregnant again for six months, a year or ever; chemo; having to do stupid 24-hour urine tests and carry 4-litre plastic containers of my own wee into the Women's Hospital every week. And I breathed out, because I wasn't there yet, and every second standing between me and a 4-litre urine container was a precious, precious thing.

Breathing in an uncomfortable spot like that can be hard, but I'd had lots of practice at it by then. I take great pride in the fact that when my brother and sister-in-law (both dive instructors) took me for my first-ever ocean scuba dive that January, I used less oxygen than either of them, despite freaking out underwater about how to clear my mask. It's not a remarkable talent—breathing—but it is a useful one.

It surprised me to find that if I didn't run away from the awfulness of my situation, I could breathe into it, explore it, feel exactly what it was like to be mother to a child who has died. This was different from being mother to a hypothetical Z, who would have been this-many months old by now, or to a hoped-for new baby, who I might conceive sometime in the future. Like it or not, neither of those babies was in my life now. All I had was Z. In that space, I thought to her, 'Well, my love. I wish you hadn't gone and died. But there's not much you can do about it now.' And in the spirit of parents whose kids have been conscripted to the army, I thought, 'I wish you didn't have this job (being dead/being "one with the universe" or whatever it is that baby souls do after they die) but I still love you and I wish you'd send me a postcard or call me sometimes.' Then I felt silly, because there was her star, which was always there twinkling at us, and the camellia tree, which burst into bloom just when my heart was breaking, and her pomegranate tree, and her roses, and the leaves in the river in Cairns, and slow-moving clouds, and the sea at Somers, and the bird noises in the bush chapel where her ashes were, and I realised I was being a pretty demanding mama.

It dawned on me that I actually know Z better now than when she was born. And if somehow my knowledge of her, and love for her, has expanded, then there *is* more Z. She is still growing, she is finding her feet in the world, even if I don't (in the way of all parents) really understand what her job entails. It isn't how I wanted my daughter to be in the world, but I know now that whatever she is doing is important, because it is important to her, and therefore to me. If I just keep demanding that she fit in with what I need (which I know she can't do anymore) then we will both feel awful, and maybe I'll miss seeing what she can do. I wish we'd had more time together in the conventional sense, but I can't be churlish about it, because it isn't her fault. And if I want to love her exactly as she is, then I have to be open to receiving her little hippy-style postcards of brightly coloured leaves and odd cloud formations.

I have a better sense now that part of my job in parenting Z is to trace where she went when she died—to resolve for myself where her little soul went, so that I can keep loving her and learning about her. When you prepare for parenthood, they don't tell you that you may need some existential philosophy. But I think that is one of my main tasks for Z. And, as far as I can tell, she is here in this world. In fact, she is in the process of reconnecting me with the world I felt so lost in after the accident.

For so long after the accident, everything felt wobbly, groundless, precarious. I was terrified about setting up rituals, in case I made promises to her that I couldn't keep: a grave neglected over the years, a name unspoken. But that was back when I thought of time as a line, and of our grief as a spot fading in the distance.

In those months after the miscarriage, something big shifted, so that I felt more settled with my grief. Where before, when I had heard people say that Z would 'always be with us', I would nod and vaguely agree; now I genuinely feel as though she is always with me. She is not stuck in the past, not defined by the trauma of the accident or the delicacy of her newborn form; nor trapped elsewhere in a 'heaven' that I don't believe in, or a far-off future moment of reunion. Instead, I carry her and my grief for her in my heart, in my cells, and I find her everywhere I go. She is woven into things right here—in the clothes and jewellery I choose each morning, the leaves of her pomegranate tree, the starry night, the little words I say quietly to myself and to her. I no longer have to choose between embracing her and being here in this life because I can exist now as her mother; as someone partially constituted by her and the love we still feel for her. I don't have to choose between life and death either, because they too are intertwined. She skips between both, playing on and around them, as though on a giant Möbius strip.

There's still sadness that she's not here in the fleshy, noisy way of other children, but I recognise that as my own small sense of not getting what I want, rather than as any failing on her part. The sadness at losing her and the joy at having her as my daughter have become stitched together, so that I can hardly tell which is which. It's specific to her, and my love for her, rather than being measurable as happy or sad. So, I'm still a bit of a weepy mess, but in an alive way rather than a broken or depressed way. This is what it means to love a dead child. You can expect nothing back in return. Yet, in accepting this, I feel like she has schooled me on living and dying.

It sounds trite to say, 'I feel more grounded now,' but I mean it literally. My child, flesh of my flesh, is buried in the ground, and so that ground is part of me too. When the soles of my feet touch the earth, I say hello to her, I tell her where I'm going. At first she was localised to that particular spot, but the rain has leached her essence and the worms have exchanged her particles, so that now I'm not sure exactly where she is—which means she exists everywhere, in a state of possibility.

Slowly, my sadness for having no more Z in my arms—and in our house, in her fleshy realness—is mingling with wonder that I can still get little peeks of her. I was walking to the shops the other day and it hit me that she might have been walking with me by now. I suddenly thought, 'Here; this is where her little hand would be, tight in my hand. Walking together.' And I could just about feel her chubby fingers, the softness of her skin, and could suddenly feel both the no more and the more at the same time. *I love you exactly as you are, my darling girl.*

•

I feel surprisingly sane, for all that has happened. I think it helped to give myself permission to go insane with grief when I needed to. Just small bits of mundane madness: smelling roses and muttering, *I love you, my little one*, into their centres, naming our new car and bestowing her with magical protective powers. And is that really insanity? Or just permission to feel the full range of human emotion—to refuse to pack certain emotions off to the loony bin?

As for my desperate searching for a solution to my grief, here is my answer: there is no answer (*sharp intake of breath*) but you are infinitely more capable of surviving and, indeed, flourishing in this groundless state than you give yourself credit for (*exhale*). This groundlessness, this suffering, this feeling that your heart will explode and that *this* is unbearable, is about as normal as it gets, and you are, in fact, able to bear it, even when it doesn't feel that way. If you can stop trying to escape long enough to pay attention, you'll notice that not only are you bearing the unbearable, but what feels monumental and unchangeable nonetheless does change moment to moment; sometime subtly, sometimes radically.

Even the mountains are not static. The shifting ground beneath us will take away everyone we love, but it will also (eventually) end all suffering. This suffering doesn't mean that something is broken or wrong with you—this is the state of being human, of being a fragile living thing. This is what it feels like to be stretched between being born and dying.

Part III
RIPPLES

28

Both my babies

When I was in the depths of grief, it seemed as though all the books I could find on perinatal death traced a similar narrative arc: baby dies, sadness ensues, then the birth of new baby restores faith in life, the universe and everything. It's a nice framing device, babies as bookends with the grief neatly contained in between. My own experience was more unruly.

Hearing all those 'happy ever afters' just felt cruel—particularly when we were trying so hard to replicate the formula, with no success. In that babyless space, I had to find something else. Mostly, it was a willingness to experience and sit with the things I wanted to run a mile from. I am now old friends with grief. I treat it with a healthy respect. On some days, it is still enormous and crushing, but at the same time has become ordinary—we fold it up with our washing and rinse it out when we brush our teeth. When I laugh, I want to know that her little cells are laughing within mine, and that when I see something beautiful, it is all the more beautiful because it feels like she is a part of it, and all the more heartbreaking because she is not here to see it.

If you are not yet in a state to hear about subsequent children, stop reading here.

•

This is our happy ever after. Three IVF cycles after the miscarriage, we got some good news. There was a positive pregnancy test, a scan with a heartbeat, and then, in May 2012, a beautiful baby boy, Ali. We still can't believe our luck. He is, as a dear friend puts it, a 'cube of joy'. Often a cube of joy that doesn't want to go to bed, or put his pants on, but a cube of joy nonetheless. He is reassuringly robust. He bellowed the moment he was born, and continues to be—which is a comfort to me—a noisy sleeper. I hope he lives to tell his own story. That sounds a morbid way to think of your child (and, indeed, the thought of losing him makes me weep regularly) but it also gives me some perspective and sharpens my gratitude for him.

I have to be honest here. Having another baby did help. As the grief settled like muddy water in a jar, I could see there were different components of differing weights within it. The specific grief for our specific daughter was sedentary, solidifying at the bottom. It is with us wherever we go, it has become part of the ground underlying everything else. I am still heartbroken that she is not here, that we will never know what she would have been like as a schoolkid, as a big sister. But the grief for not being a mother of a living child—the hankering for the ephemera of tiny socks and small seashell ears, the patting and the rocking, playing peek-a-boo, making the train-cake—I have been slowly and happily pouring away since the wintery Monday afternoon when Ali emerged screamingly alive.

And while Ali is the happy ever after to our story, as always, the story has taken some unexpected turns. Rima and I have separated—mostly for reasons pre-dating our accident—but we remain friends, and co-parents to Ali and the girls. Our universe has fractured again, but no one has fallen down the chasm this time. And there is a freedom in calling a truce, and in deciding to stop pacing through the old dance steps that sent us round in painful circles.

Both my babies

Thursday, 28 June 2012

Ali has changed so much already since he was born. Even within 24 hours of his birth, his head was no longer the soft squished newborn head, and the cord which was so plump and pulsing at his birth was quickly drying up and turning into a belly button. Too many tiny changes to catalogue—new skills, new habits, growth in every direction. He's now over a month old, and yet his birth still feels so close—the surprise of having a living baby hasn't worn off yet for me.

And it hit me that this is what being a parent is, to bear witness and care for another human being through their most intense period of growth and change—where their existing self is constantly slipping like mercury through your fingers, becoming a new baby, a new little person every day as they grow and change. As much as I want to grasp onto who Ali is this very minute, I know that this current version of him is just a snapshot—that he is the process rather than the minute by minute product of himself.

When I had that thought, it made me cry because I'm only just starting to grasp how much we missed out on with Z. Does that mean I completely missed parenting her, because, by the time I held her in my arms, she was still—she was not going to grow or move anymore? I felt lost for a moment as her mother. But not only did I love her through the constant transitions and growth of pregnancy—from a tiny cellular possibility to a kicking, hiccoughing, nearly six pound baby—I also loved her and held her through that other big transition, from life to death. I was there surrounding her as her heart slowed and then stopped as we sat in the wreckage, but I was also there after she was born, holding her as the living warmth ebbed away from her body and her little soul stretched away to begin its travels.

I asked Rima the other day whether she thought Z could hear my dad singing her a lullaby when he held her after she was born, and she said, 'Yes, the soul hangs around for a while, at least a day—that's why we stay with someone who has died, with their body for the first day.' That second transition—from someone you love whose heart has just stopped beating, to a cold body—has always frightened me a bit, thanks to all those cultural phobias of dead bodies and deterioration. There was a moment on the day we spent with her, when I had slept briefly and I woke and asked to hold her again, and the cold on her cheeks was noticeable. I knew we didn't have much time with her—that the little baby soul we loved so much was mingling back into the atmosphere and gradually relinquishing the atoms of her body back to the elements.

I look at all the beautiful cards and gifts that family and friends have sent congratulating us on Ali's birth, and it feels so unfair that Z got condolences instead. It will always be unfair. But now she exists in a state beyond fair and unfair. And to hold her as she crossed into death and to love her even all the way into death was all I could do as her mama.

Last night I dreamt that I was out shopping with Rima and the girls. We were in a toyshop, and Z was with us—she was a curly-headed toddler about fifteen months old. One moment she was looking at toys in our aisle, and the next I asked Rima where she'd gone—we couldn't see her anywhere. We were searching all over the shop, calling out her name, and when it was clear she wasn't there, we ran out to the street and were looking for her. I saw Rima run across the road and I was so scared that I'd see her pick up Z from the road—I wanted to find her but please god, not on the road, not hurt or killed.

Then a tram came, and I realised it was our tram home. I felt compelled to get on. In my head all sorts of arguments were tested and rejected—maybe she would know it was our tram, maybe someone took her on it. I had no idea, but I just needed get on that tram. Somehow we were now looking for both Ali and Z. I stepped

Both my babies

up onto the tram, searching—and there she was, running into my arms. I hugged her to me and breathed her in, simultaneously looking around for Ali. 'Who found her?' I asked. 'Was there a little boy with her?' I asked. Some lanky teenagers sitting opposite waved at me to indicate it was them who had found her. They pointed and there was Ali—himself but a toddler only a few months younger than Z. I drew him and Z in—a solid little person in each arm—sobbing with relief. 'Oh my babies,' I cried, 'I'm so sorry. I'm so sorry I took my eyes off you!'

I woke to my own crying, and found my arms around someone warm—Rima. I listened for Ali's snuffling breath in the co-sleeper next to our bed, and when I heard him, I exhaled—grateful for him; grateful for Z visiting my dreams; and so, so grateful for that feeling, however brief, of holding both my babies in my arms.

29

Zoe's Law

In mid-2013, several Sydney friends got in touch about the proposed 'Zoe's Law' bill before the New South Wales Parliament. Zoe was the name Brodie Donegan and Nick Ball gave their baby daughter, stillborn on Christmas Day 2009 after Brodie was hit by the drug-affected driver of a van, just two days before our accident. A fetal heartbeat was still present when Brodie arrived at hospital, but by the time doctors could stabilise her, it was fading, and Zoe was stillborn at thirty-two weeks gestation. As in our case, because Zoe did not show any signs of life when she was born, the driver could only be charged with dangerous driving causing grievous bodily harm, not dangerous driving causing death.[1] For Brodie and Nick, this quirk of legal personhood meant that they felt that Zoe's life was never 'acknowledged or taken into account'.[2]

When Brodie and Nick took to the media to campaign for a change to the law to recognise Zoe and other stillborn babies as legal persons for the purposes of the criminal law, it was Christian Democrat politician Reverend Fred Nile who acted first. Nile had made a name for himself by proclaiming homosexuality a 'lifestyle choice' that is 'immoral, unnatural and abnormal', seeking a moratorium on Muslim people migrating to Australia, and using the suicide of TV personality

Charlotte Dawson to publicise his (completely unfounded) theories about a link between depression and abortion.[3] Classy politics, indeed.

Without consulting Brodie and Nick, Nile used their daughter's name to introduce a private member's bill that would create a new offence of 'causing serious harm to or the destruction of a child in utero'.[4] To claim back their daughter's name, Brodie and Nick worked with their local member, Chris Spence, to launch their own private member's bill. It was more circumspect than Nile's with its pro-life undertones, but nonetheless sought to define a fetus as a legal person for the purposes of particular offences. Nile's bill would have extended legal personhood to a 'child in utero' defined as 'the prenatal offspring of a woman'—vague enough to cover an embryo from conception, and conspicuously avoiding use of the term 'fetus', which only applies from about nine weeks after conception. Spence's bill would have applied once the fetus was at least twenty-weeks gestation; or, if gestational age could not be determined, where the fetus had a body mass of 400 grams or more.

I'd avoided getting involved in the debate because I still wasn't sure exactly what I thought. Rima and I were in the midst of a divorce (when you've got kids, pets and a mortgage, I think separation still counts as a divorce, even though we'd never been able to get legally married). Ali and I were living with friends and family while we sorted out our post-separation accommodation. I was back at work, teaching a new subject, and often sleep deprived thanks to a night-waking toddler. But I knew that this was something I had to engage with—and that it was only by writing about it that I could figure out exactly what I thought about it. I'd been livid in January 2010 when a pro-lifer had sought to use our case to suggest that 'permissive abortion laws' were to blame for the law's failure to recognise the distinct harm of losing a wanted pregnancy due to someone else's violence or reckless driving. I had been deep in my grief then, and wasn't ready to cross the chasm between my grieving heart and my brain's capacity for legal reasoning.

When I revisited it all in late 2013, the thing that bothered me about the debate so far was that it had been reduced to polarised understandings of pregnancy. Either you were pro-choice, and opposed Zoe's Law because it sought to extend legal personhood to fetuses; or you saw the fetus as a 'baby', and, therefore, all babies, whether in or outside the womb, should be 'worthy' of legal personhood, even at the expense of the legal personhood or basic human rights of their mothers. In that shallow dichotomy, I could be a feminist or a grieving mother, but not both. But as I read and wrote my way around the topic, it became clear that this dichotomy had at its core some shady unstated assumptions.

First was the assumption that everything turned on the inherent characteristics of the fetus: was it human enough, or similar enough to a newborn baby, to count as a legal person? Or did women's rights to make decisions regarding their own bodies while pregnant depend on defining the fetus as 'just a bundle of cells'? Given the diversity of religious and philosophical beliefs in the world, and the diversity of situations in which pregnant women find themselves, it is unlikely that any kind of consensus will ever be reached on the inherent value of any particular fetus, let alone 'the fetus'.

This whole line of inquiry about the 'value' or 'sanctity' of the fetus as an archetype required a disembodied kind of thinking, a stripping away of the pregnant woman and the maternal–fetal relationship that makes fetal life possible. In assessing the status of 'the fetus', the mother was dissected out of the picture, reduced to mere geography. I thought of Da Vinci drawings—disembodied wombs sliced open like seedpods.

This was the kind of logic that led Alabama lawyers and judges to interpret 'environment' to include the womb—repurposing laws designed to address children being exposed to meth labs, in order to charge and convict women whose babies have been found with drugs in their system.[5] The same logic led an Alabama district attorney in 2015 to file a motion to terminate a pregnant prison inmate's parental rights over her embryo when she was in early pregnancy and wanting an abortion.[6] The case never went to trial, as the woman eventually withdrew her request for an abortion. Whether that represented her choice or a concession to the pressure placed on her will never be known. If a woman's 'parental rights' to an embryo or fetus within her own uterus can be terminated and handed over to welfare authorities, what rights are left for the rest of her? If the food she eats or drugs she inhales affect the embryo, then do the authorities also have 'parental rights' over her mouth, stomach and lungs? Her blood vessels? Imagining the fetus as a separate legal person suddenly propels us into a world like that of Margaret Atwood's dystopian novel *The Handmaid's Tale*, where women are treated as 'two-legged wombs'.

Framing the debate in terms of the inherent features of the fetus also conceded important ground. It suggested that the reason we could 'let' women make decisions about pregnancy and abortion was because those decisions were relatively inconsequential ones, which were merely about a 'bundle of cells'. When those decisions became weightier, as fetuses have a tendency to do, the arguments about women's rights to make those decisions appeared shakier.

The key difference between a late-term fetus in utero and a newborn baby is not size or stage of development; plenty of premmie babies have been born alive who were smaller and less developed than Z. Rather, it is the fetus's situation within its mother's womb and person, and its reliance on her for every possible need, that makes the question of fetal legal personhood complicated. Z had died not from any wound caused from the impact, but from the placenta abrupting and detaching from the wall of my uterus. She was left drifting, like a small astronaut whose oxygen supply has come unplugged. Her death did not make sense outside the context of my womb and my body bearing the brunt of two vehicles colliding.

I found myself agreeing with Sydney Law School academic Kristin Savell, who suggests that birth is significant because it is the moment when the baby becomes an embodied individual.[7] At birth, the baby's skin encounters not amniotic fluid or the inside of the mother's uterus, but air, and other people, and with them the social interactions that create our need for law and legal personhood. Birth is itself the division that creates a new individual, and in which the baby transitions from the universe of the uterus to our worldly, social universe. Here we interact via laws, language, social conventions and sometimes violence, rather than via the flow of nutrients across the placenta, and the muffled sounds of heartbeat, voice and bodily functions.

Savell's approach resonated with me, because in my belly, Z had been Haloumi—a mysterious baby-fetus, known only by the sensations she created within my body. We loved her, even as we guessed whether she was a she or a he, or whether that was a knee or an elbow moving across my belly. But once she was born, she solidified into herself. Yes, her face was always hers, but we didn't know it as hers until she was born and we became acquainted with the whole particularity of her. And as much as we loved Haloumi as a nickname, she was now a little person, and needed a proper person name. The fact that she died before that transition occurred—from fetus-baby to person—may have meant that the law couldn't treat *her death* as the death of a legal person, but it didn't mean the law couldn't treat *her* as a legal (but deceased) person once she *was* born, requiring a funeral and certification as our child.

I also wanted to address the pervasive assumption that legal personhood amounted to some kind of societal certification of human worth. In an increasingly secular society, law is one of the last bastions of ritual. Judges and barristers wear ceremonial robes and wigs, and the court space is a semi-sacred one where there is a time for bowing, a time for speaking, and a time for silence. And what are legal documents but magical incantations, which, when prepared, signed, sealed and certified in the correct manner, can change the unseen properties of people and things? Yet, I wanted to challenge the recourse to law, and to suggest that the task of making sense of pregnancy loss or termination is an intensely personal one, unsuited to the universal definitions and mechanisms for consistency that are the hallmarks of legal processes. I was hesitant to invite the law into my uterus—to let it mediate the shifting relationships between the unfolding process of fetal life within my body, and my developing emotional and cognitive sense of my child within my heart and mind.

When I started researching other jurisdictions that had created criminal offences around fetal deaths in utero, what shocked me was how often such laws were used to prosecute the pregnant women themselves. These were women like Melissa Rowland. Pregnant with twins in Utah in 2004, she had initially refused to consent to a caesarean section delivery, and was subsequently charged with murder when one of her twins was stillborn.[8] On a plea bargain, the prosecutor dropped the murder charge in return for her pleading guilty to child endangerment. By expanding the legal meaning of 'child' to include a fetus in utero, the Utah prosecutors construed a pregnant woman's decisions about her medical treatment and about birth as criminal acts.

Nina Buckhalter and Rennie Gibbs were Mississippi women also charged with homicide offences when their babies were stillborn. Prosecutors argued that the women's illegal drug use amounted to manslaughter by culpable negligence, in Buckhalter's case, and 'depraved heart murder', in Gibbs case. Both indictments were eventually dismissed, but only after consuming years of these young women's lives.[9]

Indiana woman Bei Bei Shuai was 33-weeks pregnant when her lover left her. Distraught and suicidal, she swallowed rat poison. She was hospitalised, survived and the pregnancy continued, but, a week later, an obstetrician noticed an unusual fetal heart rate, and Shuai consented to an emergency caesarean section. Her baby daughter, AS, was born alive, but gravely ill, due to a brain haemorrhage. Three days later, Shuai consented to removing AS from life support and she died. The coroner's view was that the brain haemorrhage was due to the rat poison. Prosecutors treated the transmission of the poison from Shuai's bloodstream, across the placenta and into her baby's bloodstream as a voluntary act of poisoning, and charged Shuai with murder and attempted feticide.[10]

I thought of these women and the hospital rooms where they had held their babies, feeling their cheeks get a little colder. I thought of how broken we were in that moment, and imagined that vulnerable space suddenly crowded by police with accusing looks, taking away our child's body as 'evidence' against us. To heap on punishments when these women had already lost so much felt more like cruelty than justice.

The acts that these women were being punished for also felt very different from the violence in cases where men stabbed or punched their pregnant partners. These were acts that concerned the women's own bodies: decisions about medical treatment, or addictive or self-harming behaviours. It was only due to the involuntary physiological processes of their own pregnant bodies that their acts affected their fetus. They couldn't insulate their fetus from their actions, their addictions or their mental illnesses any more than they could separate their minds from their bodies.

When laws are promoted as 'protecting' mothers like me and our babies but end up being used to prosecute women like Melissa Rowland, Nina Buckhalter, Rennie Gibbs or Bei Bei Shuai, it contributes to polarised views of 'good mothers' and 'bad mothers'. And it is not just the so-called 'bad mothers' who are policed by these prosecutions. These cases send a powerful message to all pregnant women that if they are not compliant when doctors advise an intervention during their pregnancy, they risk criminal charges and the shaming that comes with the 'bad mother' tag. And for those women who are pregnant and struggling with addictions or mental health difficulties, evidence from the US shows that taking a punitive approach means that these women are less likely to seek prenatal care or to disclose these complicating factors to their health care providers—resulting in worse outcomes for their babies.[11]

I sat down and nutted out a short article for *The Conversation* website.

Why losing my daughter means I don't support Zoe's Law
18 November 2013

A bill currently before the NSW Parliament attempts to criminalise harm to late-term fetuses that die due to injuries inflicted on their mother. But is fetal legal personhood the best way to recognise the particular harm of losing a much-wanted pregnancy due to someone else's violent or careless act?

As a feminist legal academic, I have professional insight into the prospective law; I also have personal insight as a mother who lost her unborn child in a car accident.

It reads like a macabre riddle—someone died within my body, and yet I live. It's one that I've puzzled (and wept) over many times since a four-wheel drive hit our station wagon when I was eight months pregnant in December 2009, causing our baby daughter to die before she could be born.

The current law's attempt to answer this riddle is a clumsy one. It characterises our daughter's death as one of my 'injuries', because she died in utero, and was not a legal 'person' with a separate existence from me at the time she died.

It is exactly this riddle which Zoe's law (No 2) attempts to resolve.

What the bill does
The bill defines a fetus over twenty weeks or weighing more than 400 grams as a legal 'person', for the purposes of dangerous driving causing grievous bodily harm and a number of other criminal offences.

Zoe's law is named after Brodie Donegan's daughter, Zoe, who also died in utero due to dangerous driving in December 2009.

For Zoe's parents, this bill seeks to close what they see as a gap in the law:

> We have never felt that Zoe's loss of life was acknowledged or taken into account ... I couldn't reconcile that the child I'd

applied for a stillbirth certificate for, held a funeral for, received the baby bonus for, received paid parental leave from work for; wasn't recognised separately to me.

The law's response touches a raw nerve because so much of the grieving process is about developing an understanding of *who* you are mourning—a process already complicated when your child dies before (or around the time of) birth.

Calling our loss an 'injury' fails to acknowledge the depth of sorrow involved in grieving a child. But is fetal legal personhood the best way for the law to recognise our loss?

Legal personhood

A key difficulty here is that legal personhood has been interpreted as the definition of human life and worth. Legal personhood is a technical category that sometimes includes non-humans, such as corporations. Its purpose is not to define human life but to enable an autonomous interaction with the law.

Legal personhood doesn't make sense for a baby in utero. The physical reality of pregnancy means that the baby is the opposite of autonomous—it depends completely on the mother and is completely contained within her body until birth.

While inside the mother, a baby is covered by her legal personhood. Birth is the moment of separation when the baby is no longer contained within the mother and her legal personhood.

I have no doubt that my daughter was a person—but I am comfortable with the idea that, at the time she died, she was protected by my legal personhood rather than her own.

Once the fetus is defined as a legal person, the law has a direct relationship with it, and the mother's consent becomes irrelevant. She becomes invisible in the eyes of the law, despite the physical realities of pregnancy meaning that any interaction with the fetus necessarily involves her.

Zoe's bill is drafted to create exceptions for anything done to the fetus by the mother, with her consent or by a medical professional. But this creates a situation where it is legal to take the life of some legal persons, but not others, depending on the consent of a third party (the mother).

And it opens up the prospect of human rights claims being brought on behalf of a fetus. With that comes the prospect of challenges to the pro-choice exceptions built into Zoe's law.

Reproductive autonomy

My own view is that the fetus is a life. But because it is a life completely contained within a legal person (the mother), any interests or rights it could have can only be advanced through the consent of the mother.

As a pregnant woman, what you choose to do with the life within you is a huge moral decision. But because that decision is completely contained within your body, and because you are already the mother to any child that might potentially be born, you are the best person to make that decision.

You are the most qualified person, the most concerned person, the person most at risk, and the most interested person.

For anyone to take that decision out of your hands, whether to insist that you continue with a pregnancy or to terminate a pregnancy against your will, is a violation. It goes beyond pain and physical injuries—it violates the mother's decision for her own body and for any potential child.

It is *this* violation that I would suggest would be a much more effective base for a law recognising the harm Brodie Donegan and I experienced.

This could involve, for example, a specific offence addressing conduct that ends the life of a fetus without the mother's consent.

Our current laws misconstrue forced pregnancy loss as just another type of bodily injury, rather than recognising it as a violation of reproductive autonomy. Like rape, forced pregnancy loss deserves its own offence centred on the notion of violation, rather than injury.

A law that frames forced pregnancy loss as a specific offence could acknowledge the family's suffering in cases like mine and Brodie's—and protect reproductive autonomy.

It doesn't resolve the heart-breaking riddle of losing a child, but I'm not sure that any law could.

•

Just three days after my piece in *The Conversation* was published, the bill passed the lower house by sixty-three votes to twenty-six. Suddenly, fetal legal personhood was no longer a speculative idea put forward by the fundamentalist pro-life fringe, but a viable prospect, and I was fielding interview requests from local and national radio and TV stations. Again, I thought of Lindy Chamberlain, but this time I had to speak both in my personal and academic capacity. I suspect many journalists initially found me a contradiction in terms: a bereaved mother who *didn't* want her child recognised as a legal person (at least while in utero). They were compassionate, though, and curious, which I was thankful for. And this was exactly the paradox I wanted to talk about—the limited usefulness of legal personhood for defining who was 'human', and the gap between diverse understandings of the emotional or relational personhood of the fetus, and the law's need to set more universal definitions and minimum standards.

In the months after the lower house vote, I was invited to speak with a number of members of the New South Wales upper house, along with the Australian Medical Association and Family Planning NSW. We sat on couches in MPs' offices, while I told my story, and the stories of women in juridictions allowing for fetal legal personhood—women like Melissa Rowland and Bei Bei Shuai.

We urged caution in passing legislation that could have unpredictable impacts on women's access to all kinds of medical treatment while pregnant, and on their ability to make decisions regarding pregnancy and birth. We talked about Angela Carder, a pregnant woman dying of cancer in Washington DC in 1987, who against her will was subjected to a caesarean at 26-weeks gestation because a court found that 'the state has [an] important and legitimate interest in protecting the potentiality of human life'. Her daughter died within two hours of the operation, and Angela two days later.[12]

We talked about Marlise Muñoz, who in November 2013 was declared brain dead in Texas, but was kept on life support machines against her express wishes and those of her family because she was fourteen weeks pregnant at the time. The hospital believed it was bound to do so by the *Texas Advance Directives Act*, which states that, 'A person may not withdraw or withhold life-sustaining treatment ... from a pregnant patient.'[13] It was over two months before Marlise's husband was able to obtain a court order both requiring the hospital to turn off the machines and holding that 'lifesaving measures' could not apply to brain-dead patients. Like my body, Marlise's had held both life and death, but in the reverse order. A 'fetal personhood' approach would suggest that the two scenarios were the same, that pregnancy involved two persons, and just because one person died, that did not require the death of the other. This was a version of pregnancy alien to that I had experienced, in which the embryo/fetus makes itself known in the early stages much as a virus would (via queasiness and weariness) and gradually accretes into a presence—not of an equal or a rival for control of my body, but of a small vulnerable being, for which I was completely responsible. When my daughter's heartbeat stopped and her brain went quiet in my womb, my survival did not require the artificial continuation of her breathing and blood circulation.

There are so many kinds of unenviable decisions to make, and being pregnant means it is impossible to separate a decision made for yourself from a decision made about your fetus. It is easy to feel cynical about politicians from a distance, but the representatives we met with took their parliamentary roles seriously, and were intent on learning as much as they could about the potential repercussions of treating a baby in utero as a legal person.

In early 2014 there were rumours there would be an upper house vote on the Zoe's Law bill, but numbers seemed to be shifting against it, and the bill's sponsors held off. In February, the bill's sponsor in the lower house, Chris Spence, stood down from parliament to face allegations before the Independent Commission Against Corruption, shortly to be followed by the bill's sponsor in the upper house, Marie Ficarra.

Meanwhile, in October 2013, a drug-affected driver misjudged the lanes on a bridge in Dapto, New South Wales, and ploughed into a hatchback containing the 32-weeks pregnant Jacqueline Sparks and her brothers. Jacqueline's uterus ruptured on impact, resulting in her daughter being stillborn and the loss of Jacqueline's uterus. After the driver who caused the accident was sentenced in October 2014, Jacqueline and her partner, Chi Nguyen, called for the New South Wales Parliament to pass the Zoe's Law bill, which had been languishing in the upper house for nearly a year. Despite their appeals, in November 2014, the Zoe's Law bill lapsed without ever having been voted on in the upper house.

In the years since the vote, the accidents, and the headlines keep coming.[14] Brodie Donegan continues to agitate for legislative change, stating in 2016, 'I believe that the current laws must be improved to adequately reflect the loss of the unborn child due to a serious criminal or violent act and acknowledge the impact that has on the entire family, rather than keeping the loss within the mother's injuries.'[15] Fred Nile introduced a new 'Zoe's Law' Bill to the New South Wales Upper House in April 2017, again without permission from Zoe's parents to use her name. Meanwhile, the decriminalisation of abortion, which was delivered in Victoria in 2008, appears stalled in New South Wales. While abortion remains on the criminal code, a Zoe's Law-type bill is likely to throw the legal status of abortion in New South Wales into confusion, with the possibility of health professionals withdrawing their provision of services, for fear of criminal charges.

Meanwhile, a Queensland mother whose daughter was stillborn in similar circumstances is agitating for a Queensland version—'Sophie's Law'. She wants 'all babies past 30 weeks gestation to have the right to be classed as a human being', but specifies that she does not 'want to affect a woman's right to abortion or have a pregnancy terminated for any medical reasons'.[16]

There is a persistence here—in the women who want their and their family's loss acknowledged, in strong public support for their campaigns; and in the heartbreaking frequency of pregnancy loss resulting from criminal behaviour, particularly driving offences. This issue is not going to disappear of its own accord. Their babies' names haunt us. And this, I guess, is partly the reason these families persist with their campaigns to change the law. Our babies' names did not end up on child care waiting lists, on school rolls, on excursion slips or birthday invitations. If anyone but our loved ones is to remember them, it is up to us. We do not want their names, their little lives and the big dreams we had for them to die with us. If we have to live without them, we want something to come of this grief—that it might reduce the chances of other babies and families suffering a similar fate, or at least of suffering the indignity of the loss of their child being treated as an 'injury'. But the last thing I would want my daughter remembered for would be for laws that had the effect (intended or not) of winding back women's reproductive rights and ability to access medical treatment during pregnancy. Or, worse still, laws that flattened the complexities of pregnancy, maternal health, and addiction into two categories: 'bad mothers', who should be punished for potentially harming their babies in utero; and 'good mothers', who were willing and compliant gestators, always prioritising fetal life above their own.

30

Holding the torch

I had such good intentions in writing this book. I wanted to give something to newly grieving parents, to say, *You are not alone in this devastated landscape.* There are so many of us here with you, and, despite the devastation, this is still a beautiful place. We have walked it. Here is my fragile map, here is where the path emerges, here is how the parts relate to one another. It is frightening, it is painful; yet, it also inspires awe in its devastation. Unexpectedly exquisite things grow here, things you would never know about had you not set foot in the devastation. And if you can keep putting one foot in front of the other, the mud firms into a path beneath your feet, rains wash away the dirt from your body, you find debris from which to build a shelter, and, after a time, you start to notice small signs of life.

What I'd forgotten, of course, is that in the beginning, you can't see any of that because your eyes are so puffed with tears that they can hardly open. Even if you can open them and blink away the salt, you'd have to peel your hands from your face, the hands that are the only things keeping your head from hitting the floor with a dull thump. I am remembering all of this because we have, this week, been ordered back to that devastated landscape.

My sister's firstborn baby girl blows bubbles in her sleep, wrapped in layers of flannel, tubes and cords intruding on her soft skin. Her condition doesn't have a name yet; letters and numbers hover menacingly above her clear perspex box like a fatal bingo call. Whatever the ultimate order of the numbers, the real damage is being done in her cells, where her mitochondria—tiny molecular engines within each of her cells—are stalling. Not all of them, and not all at once, but for each one that stalls (one test says 78 per cent, but that may just be of her blood cells), a cell is deprived of the energy it requires for muscle activation, for digestion, or for production of proteins. Whatever the cell's purpose, it is short-changed, and her body has to work harder to achieve the same result.

She frowns, sighs wearily. Her blood shows high lactate levels, as though she is running a half-marathon rather than just lying there. Her heart is working so hard, it is enlarged, stretched. Sometimes it too gets tired, and slows. Alarms go off, the nurse comes. She presses the button quickly, then loosens the flannel layers, talks gently to her—'Hey, little one'—turns her on her side, and pats her small bottom firmly until the numbers on the heart rate monitor rise, and we all start to breathe again.

It has already been such a hard road for Mia, my tiny flannel-wrapped niece. An early evacuation from my sister's womb due to her alarmingly small size, then a transfer to the Children's Hospital with a gut infection and a heart murmur; so much prodding and poking as the doctors cajoled the secrets of her illness out of her body.

And now that they are decoding those secrets, it looks like it will be a short road too. At first they said she might live to two; then twelve months, if she's lucky. Even that may be optimistic.

So here I am, back in the wasteland, making the same wordless sounds, stepping through the familiar script of denial, anger, sadness, magical thinking. The pain doubles when I think of my sister and her pain, of her and my brother-in-law's tenderness with their fragile little daughter. Could this really be coincidence? That my mother, my sister and I all lose our firstborn daughter? I know that this is magical thinking, I know that these losses are pure dumb misfortune, but that doesn't stop my brain spinning theories, trying to construct sense from the senseless, to find a plot line or a moral for the story.

I hold my sister tight. Sob into her shoulder and try to hold firm for her sobs. I want to give my sister all that she gave me in my most broken hour, I want to give her everything I wish I'd known. But, despite the familiarity, this is a different wasteland. My map turns to soggy tissue in my hand.

I tell my law students that the value of a good set of study notes isn't the content. You can have the most accurate and concise notes but they won't help you a bit if you haven't developed them (or at least worked through them) yourself. The value is in the process of boiling down notes into summaries, of banging your head against the law, getting confused and then getting a little bit clearer. Grief is the same. I can spill the beans on what makes sense for me—on the mechanics of my beliefs about where Z is, how I honour her in my day-to-day life, how I let the grief move through me, like a sneeze, when it appears these days, intense but short-lived. Whatever your loss, I want to make it easier for you, to help you short-cut through the pain and the banging of one's head against the finality of death. But my mechanics work because I have crafted them for my own head, custom-built them around my irregularly shaped heart. Yours will be different. Just know I am here with you, holding the torch.

She was cremated, you see

Not many people
have a baby daughter who is a star.

The light and heat released
with her little five pound eight body
is still travelling
through the heavens
will bounce,
and one day light upon
someone's eye
as the light from a star.

Not many people (I like to think)
have a baby daughter who is an ocean
(and at the same time, rain).

Her water atoms
went up like a mist
found new friends
among the atoms
of other babies
grandmas
well-loved dogs.
And though it was scary to fall
(as rain)
when they hit the ocean
it felt like home.

(I like to think) Not many people
have a baby daughter who is a ballerina-shaped fuschia bud.

Her nutrients—every molecule that made
her soft skin
her fingers grip
has gifted itself to the earth
(I wouldn't have been so generous)
except for a few of the most beautiful
which circulate still in my blood.
'You have a daughter,' they say
each time they get pumped through my heart.
'You have a daughter,' they say
as they tend my broken cells.

The others
(there are millions)
find themselves
pulsing along a green stem
willing a bud to open,
feeding the thing that colours the petal,
scenting the pollen dust,
unfurling the leaf.
Are chewed on or breathed in by
living things,
And find a new home in them.

She is here.
Here.
Here a thousand times but also everywhere.
She makes me weep
at how clever and beautiful she is
And at my own small flimsy wish
For a more conventional baby.
(Still her—but here in the more conventional way)

It takes a very still
clear nightful of stars
or a big stormy oceanful of ocean
for me to know
(again, as I've always known)
how many babies it takes
to make up the sky.
Cremated and uncremated.
Missed and kissed.
Sung to and unsung to.
Innumerable,
visible
and each such a particular
little pinprick of light.

(August 2011)

Acknowledgements

With each ripple that the accident sent into our lives, I was lucky to have loved ones and strangers offering kindness and support—from the people who stopped to help and called the ambulances, the emergency workers who freed me and got us all to hospital, all the health care providers (even the physiotherapists) who worked hard to help us survive, heal and grieve, to the friends who moved furniture for us, brought us food, sent gifts and good thoughts and who continue to remember our daughter with us. My midwives (and now dear friends) Jen and Mandy—what incredible work you do, and what a difference you made!

Special thanks go to my family, particularly Mum, Dad, Erica, Jeremy, Deb, Jazzie, Jackie and Rima, as well as Penelope Goodes, for being there both in the living and the writing, every step of the way. I love you all so much and I'm so thankful you are in my life.

Belinda Quantock, Steve Macmillan, Matt Drummond, Rosalind Hearder and Samantha Kimpton and Sabdha and Cristi Pink-Charlton—thank you for providing friendship, encouragement, practical help and sage advice.

So many of the insights that made our loss bearable came from other baby lost parents who I've come to think of as my 'dead baby parents group', both at the SANDS Thornbury group and online, particularly Angie, Sally, Catherine, Merry, Jeanette, Kate, Sarah and Kate. As sorry as I am that we have this in common, I am so glad I found you. Karin and

Acknowledgements

Ned, thank you for letting me tell a piece of Albie and Esther's story, and Brigette, for sharing your experience with Sacha.

This book would not have happened without the Somers friends who encouraged me to be brave and realise I wanted to really write it. And it was Maria Tumarkin's excellent Creative Non-Fiction course put on by Writers Victoria which helped kickstart it. That course also led me to my fabulous writing group—Debi Hamilton, Frank Golding, Kath McKay and Anastasia Kanjere. Thank you for providing a structure and a space for me to build this book, one chapter at a time, and for unfailingly helpful questions, feedback and advice. Thanks also to Madeline Hamilton, for reading early fragments and encouraging me to take it further, and to the amazing Monica Dux, for taking a chance on my writing in *Mothermorphosis*, and for wise advice and playing fairy godmother to the project ever since.

Colleagues and the head of the Law School at La Trobe, Patrick Keyzer have been incredibly supportive in helping me find a middle space between what I had experienced and my legal academic writing, particularly Laura Griffin, Kirsty Duncanson and Fiona Kelly. Thank you to the various 'Shut up and Write' groups at La Trobe, Melbourne Law School and RMIT who egged me on, provided valuable feedback about the title and other key decisions about the book, and who allowed me to literally shut up and write.

For bringing it to publication and making it a better manuscript, thank you so much to Dina Kluska, Sally Heath and Louise Stirling at MUP, Sarina Rowell for sensitive and careful copyediting, Klarissa Pfisterer for working with us to develop such a beautiful cover, Nicholas Purcell for the profile photography, Paul Smitz for your proofreading, Hilary Harper, for reading closely and for her own beautiful writing, and my literary agent Clare Forster for wonderfully astute advocacy and advice.

Last but not least, thank you to my beautiful children—to Ali, for shining such light into our lives and persistently harassing me about 'finishing my chapter', and to Zainab, for teaching me about life, death and being a mother.

Notes

Chapter 1   Sunday 27 December 2009
1. *JM v QFG, GK and State of Queensland* [1997] QADT 5 (31 January 1997); *MW & Ors v Royal Women's Hospital & Ors Mw, Dd, Ta & Ab v Royal Women's Hospital, Freemasons Hospital and Victoria* [1997] HREOCA 6 (5 March 1997). The Queensland decision on direct discrimination was, however, overturned by the Queensland Supreme Court in October 1997, and the decision on indirect discrimination was remitted back to the Queensland Anti-Discrimination Commission: *QFG and GK v JM* (Ambrose J, Supreme Court of Queensland, 24 October 1997).

Chapter 6   Frida and me
1. Hayden Herrera, *Frida Kahlo: The Paintings*, Bloomsbury, 1992.

Chapter 10   The 'born alive' rule
1. *Attorney General's Reference No 3 of 1994* [1998] AC 245.
2. *Attorney General's Reference No 3 of 1994* [1998] AC 245, 269.
3. Adrian Lowe, 'Mother vows to fight on for law change over road death of unborn child', *The Age* (25 January 2010), 5.
4. *Crimes Act 1958* (Vic) s15.
5. [2003] NSWCCA 399.
6. *R v King* [2004] NSWCCA 444 (7 December 2004) at [30] per McColl JA.
7. *R v King* [2004] NSWCCA 444 (7 December 2004) at [31] per McColl JA.
8. *R v King* [2004] NSWCCA 444 (7 December 2004) at [32] per McColl JA.
9. *R v King* [2004] NSWCCA 444 (7 December 2004) at [39] per McColl JA.
10. *R v King* [2003] NSWCCA 399 (19 December 2003), [14] Tupman DCJ quoted in [10] and [14] of Spiegelman CJ's judgment.
11. *R v King* [2003] NSWCCA 399 (19 December 2003), [96].
12. Adrian Lowe, 'Mother vows to fight on for law change over road death of unborn child', *The Age* (25 January 2010), 5.
13. ibid.

Notes

Chapter 20   Heartbeat
1   http://www.sciencedirect.com/science/article/pii/S0006291X04023824.

Chapter 22   Close up with hope
1   Pema Chödrön, *When Things Fall Apart—Heart Advice for Difficult Times*, Shambhala, Boston 2000, pages 44 and 41.
2   Pema Chödrön, *When Things Fall Apart—Heart Advice for Difficult Times*, Shambhala, Boston 2000, page 53.

Chapter 23   The charnel ground
1   Pema Chödrön, *When Things Fall Apart—Heart Advice for Difficult Times*, Shambhala, Boston 2000, page 124.

Chapter 29   Zoe's Law
1   In Victoria, the charge is referred to as 'dangerous driving causing serious injury': *Crimes Act 1958* (Vic), s 15, as amended by *Abortion Law Reform Act* 2008 (Vic) s 10(2). For NSW, see: *Crimes Act 1900* (NSW), s 4, as amended by *Crimes Amendment (Grievous Bodily Harm) Act 2005* (NSW).
2   Brodie Donegan, 'In the eyes of the law, her daughter's death doesn't count' (18 September 2013), *Mamamia*, http://www.mamamia.com.au/social/zoes-law/
3   Fred Nile (27 May 2013), 'Religion, marriage & euthanasia', *Q&A* (transcript). Australian Broadcasting Corporation; 'Stop Muslim immigration, NSW Christian Democrats say', *ABC News*, Australia, 11 March 2007, http://www.smh.com.au/lifestyle/celebrity/fred-nile-under-fire-for-facebook-post-about-charlotte-dawson-abortion-20140224-33bol.html.
4   *Crimes Amendment (Zoe's Law) Bill 2013* (NSW), proposed s 41AA(1).
5   It was only in 2016 that the law was amended to clarify that this law excluded women who had taken legally prescribed drugs. Nina Martin, 'Alabama lawmakers limit drug prosecutions in pregnancy', *ProPublica* (4 May 2016), https://www.propublica.org/article/alabama-lawmakers-limit-drug-prosecutions-in-pregnancy.
6   Victoria Law, 'Alabama case illustrates difficulties women behind bars face when seeking abortion', *Rewire* (5 August 2015), https://rewire.news/article/2015/08/05/alabama-case-illustrates-difficulties-women-behind-bars-face-seeking-abortion/.
7   Kristin Savell, 'Is the "born alive" rule outdated and indefensible?' (2006), 28 *Sydney Law Review*, 625, 664.
8   *State v Rowland*, No. 041901649 (Utah Dist. Ct.-3d Apr. 7, 2004) (Fuchs J).
9   Nina Martin, 'A stillborn child, a charge of murder and the disputed case law on "fetal harm"', *ProPublica* (18 March 2014) https://www.propublica.org/article/stillborn-child-charge-of-murder-and-disputed-case-law-on-fetal-harm. See also the Alabama Supreme Court's decision in *Ex parte Ankrom No. 1110176*, 2013 WL 135748 (Ala. January 11, 2013).
10 *Bei Bei Shuai v State*, 966 N E 2d 619 (May, Najam, Riley JJ) (Indiana Court of Appeals, 2012). After significant public protests, in August 2013, the prosecutor

offered Ms Shuai a plea bargain. She pleaded guilty to criminal recklessness and was immediately released, having already served more than the maximum sentence. National Advocates for Pregnant Women, 'Thank you! Bei Bei Shuai is free!' (6 August 2013), http://advocatesforpregnantwomen.org/blog/2013/08/thank_you_bei_bei_shuai_is_fre.php.

11 Barry M Lester and Jean E Twomey, 'Treatment of substance abuse during pregnancy' (2008), 4 *Womens Health* 67, 74. Similarly, the Intergovernmental Committee of Drugs found that punitive attitudes were an 'impediment' to responding more effectively to fetal alcohol spectrum disorders: Lucinda Burns et al. (eds), *'Fetal Alcohol Disorders in Australia: An update' (Monograph of the Intergovernmental Committee of Drugs Working Party of Fetal Alcohol Spectrum Disorders, June 2012)* [2012], 76.

12 Angela Carder's family, via her estate, successfully appealed the decision after her death, in the District of Columbia Court of Appeals 573 A.2d 1235 (1990).

13 *Texas Health and Safety Code* s 166.049.

14 http://www.perthnow.com.au/news/western-australia/hundreds-farewell-crash-victim-shona-caley-and-her-unborn-child-at-corrigin-funeral/news-story/08b1cd0892a0215130d36dd515203652; http://www.smh.com.au/nsw/marco-silvestri-jailed-for-crash-that-killed-unborn-baby-20141022-119rpg.html; http://www.news-mail.com.au/news/unborn-baby-killed-car-crash/2638355/; http://www.news.com.au/lifestyle/parenting/babies/sophies-law-mother-fights-for-unborn-babies-to-be-protected-after-a-car-crash-claimed-her-daughters-life-days-from-birth/news-story/cf6f9424b2522fec0b05ba32bd3cd494; http://www.northernstar.com.au/news/unborn-baby-killed-queensland-traffic-crash/2370046/.

15 http://www.dailytelegraph.com.au/newslocal/central-coast/we-owe-it-to-zoe-to-fight-for-criminal-law-change/news-story/7e1365ac002321acf979911ad75473dd.

16 https://www.change.org/p/attorney-general-please-bring-in-sophie-s-law-to-protect-all-unborn-babies-post-30-weeks-gestation; https://www.9now.com.au/a-current-affair/2016/clip-cijyzzrok00bxb5p5r9mm81nj